CAERPHILLY COUNTY BOROUGH

3 8030 08201 2223

C000001474

Beginning
Criminal Law

Whether y   new to higher education, coming to legal study for the first time or just
wonderin   t Criminal Law is all about, **Beginning Criminal Law** is the ideal
introducti   help you hit the ground running. Starting with the basics and an overview of
each topi   ll help you come to terms with the structure, themes and issues of the
subject so   you can begin your Criminal Law module with confidence.

Adopting   and simple approach with legal vocabulary explained in a detailed
glossary,   Carr and Maureen Johnson break the subject of Criminal Law down using
practical,   y examples to make it understandable for anyone, whatever their
backgrou   ams and flowcharts simplify complex issues, important cases are
identified   ained and on-the-spot questions help you recognise potential issues or
debates v   law so that you can contribute in classes with confidence.

Beginnin   al Law is an ideal first introduction to the subject for LLB, GDL or ILEX
students   cially international students, those enrolled on distance-learning courses
or on othe   e programmes.

Claudia   nd Maureen Johnson are both lecturers in Criminal Law at the University
of Hertfor   Maureen is a senior lecturer and has been module leader on both the
undergra   LLB) and postgraduate (GDL) criminal modules for the past six years.
Claudia has had ten years' experience in criminal defence private practice and has been
teaching on both criminal teams with Maureen since 2002.

Beginning the Law

A new introductory series designed to help you master the basics and progress with confidence.

Publishing Spring 2013:

Beginning Constitutional Law, Nick Howard
Beginning Contract Law, Chris Monaghan and Nicola Monaghan
Beginning Criminal Law, Claudia Carr and Maureen Johnson
Beginning Equity and Trusts, Mohamed Ramjohn

Following in Spring 2014:

Beginning Employment Law, James Marson
Beginning Evidence, Chanjit Singh Landa
Beginning Human Rights, Howard Davis

www.routledge.com/cw/beginningthelaw

Beginning Criminal Law

CLAUDIA CARR
and
MAUREEN JOHNSON

Routledge
Taylor & Francis Group

LONDON AND NEW YORK

First published 2013
by Routledge
2 Park Square, Milton Park, Abingdon, Oxon OX14 4RN

Simultaneously published in the USA and Canada
by Routledge
711 Third Avenue, New York, NY 10017

Routledge is an imprint of the Taylor & Francis Group, an informa business

© 2013 Claudia Carr and Maureen Johnson

The right of Claudia Carr and Maureen Johnson to be identified as authors of this work has been asserted
by them in accordance with sections 77 and 78 of the Copyright, Designs and Patents Act 1988.

All rights reserved. No part of this book may be reprinted or reproduced or utilised in any form or by any electronic,
mechanical, or other means, now known or hereafter invented, including photocopying and recording, or in any
information storage or retrieval system, without permission in writing from the publishers.

Trademark notice: Product or corporate names may be trademarks or registered trademarks, and are used only for
identification and explanation without intent to infringe.

British Library Cataloguing in Publication Data
A catalogue record for this book is available from the British Library

Library of Congress Cataloging in Publication Data
A catalog record for this book has been requested

ISBN: 978–0–415–69066–9 (hbk)
ISBN: 978–0–415–69067–6 (pbk)
ISBN: 978–0–203–38567–8 (ebk)

Typeset in Vectora LH
by RefineCatch Limited, Bungay, Suffolk

CAERPHILLY COUNTY BOROUGH COUNCIL	
3 8030 08201 2223	
Askews & Holts	25-Apr-2013
345.42	£19.99
LIB1104	

Printed and bound in Great Britain by
TJ International Ltd, Padstow, Cornwall

To Ella and Hannah Rose – for
Love and Laughter.
(Claudia Carr)

For Mal. And for Saul and Luke – my best work.
(Maureen Johnson)

Contents

Table of Cases

Table of Legislation

Preface

Criminal law is often a favourite subject for law students, both in A level and undergraduate programmes. It deals with human stories – acts and emotions that everyone can appreciate and empathise with. The case law is often memorable, if sometimes unpleasant, and criminal law fills the television news and the daily paper. It is all around us.

Beginning Criminal Law has been written to provide a straightforward introduction to this fascinating subject, free of over-complication and legal jargon but covering all the principle concepts and offences taught in most undergraduate degrees. It incorporates pedagogical features such as examples, flow charts and diagrams to assist with student assimilation of relevant knowledge and includes Key Cases and Chapter Summaries as well as suggestions for further reading for each topic so that the interested reader can take their studies further.

Criminal law is a rapidly moving area of law and this edition covers the latest principles, such as the amended partial defences to murder in the Coroners and Justice Act 2009 and the January 2012 Court of Appeal judgment in *R v Clinton* which clarifies the law relating to sexual infidelity and the partial defence of loss of control. Legal updates and further comments will be made available on a regular basis on the Routledge companion website.

Both of the authors have lectured on criminal law at undergraduate and postgraduate level for a number of years, having great experience of the law and teaching. This book, with its clear learning outcomes and clear, flowing text is an ideal start for the law student or simply the interested observer of the English criminal system.

We wish to express our sincere gratitude to Fiona Briden, Damian Mitchell and the rest of their team at Routledge for overseeing the preparation and production of this text. We are also extremely grateful for the constructive and detailed feedback we received from the reviewers who evaluated draft chapters in the course of writing.

Claudia Carr and Maureen Johnson
September 2012

Guide to the Companion Website

www.routledge.com/cw/beginningthelaw

Visit the *Beginning the Law* Website to discover a comprehensive range of resources designed to enhance your learning experience.

Answers to on-the-spot questions
Podcasts from the authors provide pointers and advice on how to answer the on-the-spot questions in the book.

Online Glossary
Reinforce your legal vocabulary with our online glossary flashcards. The flashcards can be used online, or downloaded for reference on the go. Key terms are emboldened throughout the book, and you will find a deck of simple and easy to understand definitions of all of these terms for each chapter of the book here.

Case Flashcards

Test your knowledge of the key cases with this deck of flashcards which could be used to identify either the case name from the precedent set or the precedent from the case name. The flashcards can be used online, or downloaded for revision on the go.

Weblinks

Discover more with this set of online links to sources of further interest. These include links to contemporary news stories, editorials and articles, illuminating key issues in the text.

Updates

Twice a year, our authors provide you with updates of the latest cases, articles and debates within the law, so you can be confident you will always keep on track with the very latest developments.

Chapter 1
Introduction to criminal law

LEARNING OBJECTIVES

By the end of this chapter you should be able to:

- Understand why the criminal law exists
- Demonstrate a basic understanding of the principles
- Understand how and where a criminal prosecution is begun
- Have some understanding of the court process

The most appropriate starting point in a book on criminal law is to consider what a crime is. Simply defined, a crime is a public wrong, one that adversely affects society as a whole. It is an act that so offends society's standards of acceptable behaviour that it is appropriate to punish the offender rather than to compensate the aggrieved party. This chapter provides the reader who has no previous understanding of the criminal law to understand basic principles relating to what amounts to a crime, the elements of a criminal offence, sentencing and a brief introduction to the court process. Subsequent chapters discuss more substantive offences as well as defences and the subject areas identified are those that most undergraduate and postgraduates courses teach. Students should always remember that many of the areas interconnect. For example, you may be required to consider the offence of murder and the defence of self defence in a single exam question. We begin by considering the more philosophical approach to the criminal law.

CAUSING HARM TO OTHERS

John Stuart Mill, the English philosopher *(On Liberty and other writings* (1859)*)* explained that actions of individuals should not be restricted by society except where it is necessary to prevent harm being inflicted on others.

> The only purpose for which power can rightfully be exercised over any member of a civilised society against his will, is to prevent harm to others.

Mill explains that society should not interfere with another person's free choice unless that person's behaviour harms society.

There is little doubt we agree that the State should intervene to protect us when harm is caused but what is harm? Is harm caused to the individual or to society as a whole? Arguably, the two appear linked, if harm is caused to an individual, then society suffers as well. Harm has to be such that it threatens the mere fabric of society. Restricting harm caused to the individual protects not only the individual but invariably protects society – therefore an individual's restriction of behaviour can be justified where the greater good is concerned.

It is for society to determine what constitutes 'harm'. In a democratic society this should pose little difficulty. We all accept murder, rape, manslaughter, robbery, burglary and theft are all acts which are clearly wrong. Here, the victim should be protected from the 'wrong' and the wrongdoer should be punished. However, even here morals (which we look at shortly) play a role. For example, we all agree theft is wrong; harm is caused if I steal a wallet from the person sitting next to me on the train. Harm is caused to the individual and society needs to be protected from my actions! Compare my act to the single unemployed mum who steals a pint of milk and a loaf of bread to feed her family. Is harm caused here? Is her act equally as reprehensible as mine? We all know one should not steal but does society really need protection from her? Arguably not. Although the quality of the act is the same the motives are very different. Although motives play no role in criminal law, this simple example shows there are varying differing standards as to what amounts to an act that causes harm. Not only is this dependent on the morals of those who represent our 'society' but it is also largely dependent on society's expectations and the changing values of that society.

Example

Section 2(1) of the Suicide Act 1961 states that it is a criminal offence to aid, abet, counsel or procure another's suicide. Marian suffers from a terminal degenerative condition and wants her husband to be able to help her end her life at the time of her choosing, when she no longer feels her life is worth living. The law states that what she most desires – the chance to end her life with the help and support of her loving husband – is illegal. Her individual rights are curtailed in order to protect the vulnerable of society who may feel pressurised to end their life prematurely (see *R (Pretty) v DPP* (2001)). This may seem to be an acceptable approach, as harm could be caused to many if assisted suicide were permitted. One can also argue that harm is caused to Marian since her autonomous wish to end her life at the time of her choosing is denied. Hence, who is harmed is often not as straightforward as it might, at first glance, appear.

MORALITY

So far we have seen that 'harm' is a difficult concept to attempt to define. There is little doubt that morality plays a significant part in the development of the criminal law. Again, morality is a tricky term to define and it is often guided by the standards of the particular culture one studies. For example, female genital circumcision is an accepted practice in parts of Africa, most commonly in Northern Eastern parts, but here in the UK it is morally unacceptable and now, since the Female Genital Mutilation Act 2003, unlawful.

The law in England and Wales permits us to consent to a certain level of self-harm (see Chapter 7), for example, we can consent to tattooing and all forms of exotic body piercing even though we may not all find it attractive, or even acceptable.

However, there are areas of harm where the law has intervened and the case below illustrates how the law can impose its moral stamp of authority.

KEY CASE: *Brown* [1993] 2 All ER 75

Facts:

- The appellants enthusiastically engaged in acts of sado-masochism.
- Many of the acts involved personal and intimate violence.
- They are conducted in private, all parties consented and no harm was caused as a result.

Held:

The appellants were charged and convicted of actual bodily harm. They appealed but their convictions were upheld. Lord Templeman observed 'Society is entitled and bound to protect itself against a cult of violence. Pleasure derived from the infliction of pain is an evil thing. Cruelty is uncivilised.'

The court's decision clearly sends out the message that personal freedoms considered morally unacceptable can be curtailed by the courts, even where the activity is conducted in private and no harm is caused.

Contrast *Brown* with *Wilson* below.

KEY CASE: *Wilson* [1996] 3 WLR 125

Facts:

- The appellant had brandished his initials on his wife's buttocks with her consent.
- She required medical attention following an infection.
- Her husband was charged with assault occasioning actual bodily harm contrary to s 47 of the Offences against the Person Act 1861.

Held:

The husband's conviction was overturned.

The court opined that this was an act of love between husband and wife, and consensual activity between two loving partners should not be a matter for the courts.

What is the real difference between the cases? In *Wilson* injury was caused (albeit minor) and Mrs Wilson required medical attention. No such injury was caused in *Brown. Brown* involved activities which involve sexual gratification; in contrast, Mr Wilson did not receive any sexual gratification. In reality, *Brown* is a judgment where morals were examined and statements made as to how people should behave. The activities of a minority group of people with a tendency to alternative sexual acts were not the kind of activities that the court concluded could be either accepted as 'normal' or acceptable and hence they were criminalised.

The judgment's principle is reflected by Sir Patrick Devlin in *The Enforcement of Morals* as he explains:

> The criminal law is not a statement of how people ought to behave; it is a statement of what can happen to them if they do not behave; good citizens are not expected to come within reach of it or to set their sights by it, and every enactment should be framed accordingly.

WHAT IS PUNISHMENT AND WHY DO WE HAVE IT?

One of the interesting aspects of a study of the criminal law, in contrast with other areas of law, is that the criminal law seems almost tangible. Turn on the television and there will invariably be a drama, news item or media portrayal of some offence being committed. The same applies to punishment. Sometimes we might even consider that punishment of criminal offences is glamorised by the media.

In contrast to the civil law, where compensation between the parties is sufficient, a victim of a criminal offence might, quite rightly, be offended if the State suggested that compensation was an adequate remedy between the parties.

The State punishes the wrongdoer in order to enforce boundaries of acceptable behaviour. It is also a form of *'retributive justice'* where the offender must face the consequences of his undesirable activities. Retribution was one of the main principles behind the Conservative Government's reform of sentencing: *Crime, Justice and Protecting the Public* (1990).

Punishment is a form of *deterrent* which allows others to appreciate the consequences of their potential actions through the punishment of others. A custodial sentence is the ultimate deterrent, reserved for offences where a period of imprisonment and deprivation of liberty satisfies the State that justice is seen to be done.

Punishment also seeks to *rehabilitate,* reform and re-educate the offender in the hope they will not re-offend. In the situation of a relatively minor drug offence, for example, sentencing the defendant to community service together with attendance at a drug rehabilitation unit (if he shows a desire to rid the habit) could be an effective tool. The aim is to rehabilitate the offender, together with some form of punishment for the offence committed. However, rehabilitation is often difficult to achieve with re-offending rates particularly high. Where an offender is released from a short custodial sentence of under 12 months, the rate of re-offending can, according to the Ministry of Justice, *Compendium of Reoffending Statistics and Analysis May 2011*, be as high as 70 per cent. The rate is lower for sentences of between two and four years, where the offender has been given a greater opportunity to rehabilitate. Those who re-offend cite a lack of a place to live and unemployment as the main reasons for re-offending.

The State must also consider *protecting the public* where sentencing is concerned. Whilst originally this may have been achieved by the death penalty, modern-day protection is achieved by imposing lengthy prison sentences. If the offender is not in custody, electronic tagging can restrict an offender's movements whilst, at the same time, protecting the public by prohibiting the offender from visiting a particular area between certain times. Sometimes the offender is forbidden to visit particular areas, especially if the area is connected with the original offence. The benefit of electronic tagging is that it is less costly than caring for an offender in custody, but at the same time it acts as a deterrent because if the defendant breaches the conditions of his tagging he can be imprisoned for the breach.

The Human Rights Act 1998 – the Act incorporates the provisions of the European Convention of Human Rights into domestic law with effect from October 2000. By virtue of s 6, the onus is on public authorities (for example, the courts, prisons and the police) to ensure that all legislation is compatible, as far as possible, with the Convention rights. Save for the case of *Lambert* [2002] QB 112, which concerned the reverse burden of proof and the use of

Article 6, it would be reasonable to say that terrorism offences (more so than other offences we deal with in this book) have most frequently engaged use of the Convention rights.

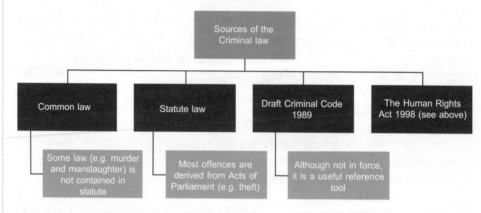

Figure 1.1 Sources of the criminal law

ELEMENTS OF CRIMINAL LIABILITY

Criminal liability is traditionally expressed in the following Latin maxim *'actus non facit reum nisi mens sit rea'* which can be translated as 'an act does not make a man guilty of a crime unless his mind is also guilty'.

We examine these terms in detail in Chapters 2 and 3, and here we simply need to outline the basic elements. Most criminal offences require both a guilty act (*actus reus*) and a guilty mind (*mens rea*) and in order for the defendant to be convicted of a criminal offence, the prosecution must prove these two elements. We will see that some offences (known as strict liability offences) only require proof of the *actus reus*, but this is an exception to the rule.

It is important to be able to identify the *actus reus* and the *mens rea* in an offence. The majority of offences are contained within statute. There are a few offences which are common law offences so the *actus reus* and *mens rea* can be found in accepted definitions of the offence, for example, the offence of murder.

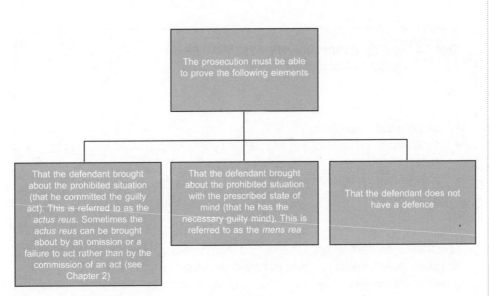

Figure 1.2 The elements of a criminal offence

The burden of proof

The burden of proof is on the prosecution to prove the *mens rea* and the *actus reus* of the offence beyond reasonable doubt. This means the jury must be satisfied so they are sure that the defendant committed the offence he is being tried for. If they are not sure, or there is any element of doubt, the defendant must be acquitted.

The prosecution must also prove that the defendant cannot rely on a defence. Thus, the defendant does not have to prove anything at all. He can simply wait and watch whilst the State (who prosecute) accuses the defendant and then sets out to prove its case. The well-worn phrase that the 'defendant is innocent until proven guilty' is entirely accurate. It is for the prosecution to prove its case, not for the defendant to disprove the case or assert his innocence.

The authority for the principle that the prosecution must prove the *mens rea* and *actus reus* beyond reasonable doubt is illustrated in the case below.

KEY CASE: *Woolmington v DPP* **[1935] All ER 1**

Facts:

- Mr and Mrs W separated.
- Mr W wished to persuade Mrs W to return by threatening to kill himself with a shotgun.
- Accidentally, the shotgun went off and he killed his wife.

Held:

At first instance, the trial judge misdirected the jury stating that once the *actus reus* had been proved, the *mens rea* of murder could be presumed unless the defendant proved to the contrary. Mr W was convicted of her murder.

The House of Lords overturned his conviction on the basis that the onus was on the prosecution to prove the killing was not accidental. Lord Sankey LC held as follows:

> Throughout the web of English criminal law one golden thread is always to be seen – that is the duty of the prosecution to prove the prisoner's guilt . . .

> No matter what the charge or where the trial, the principle that the prosecution must prove the guilt of the prisoner is part of the common law of England and no attempt to whittle it down can be entertained.

The standard of proof

The standard of proof rests with the prosecution to prove the defendant's guilt beyond reasonable doubt, referred to as the 'golden thread' by Lord Sankey LC above. This contrasts with civil law where the standard of proof is satisfied on a balance of probabilities, that is, 51 per cent. In criminal law, however, the standard of proof is set considerably higher. The justification for this can be found in the differing penalties that can be imposed on a civil defendant found liable and the criminal defendant convicted of a criminal offence. Since the penalty in civil law tends to be damages (compensation) between the parties, this form of 'punishment' tends to pale into insignificance when compared to the possible penalties in criminal law. The defendant could be fined (drawing a parallel with civil law), but this will also result in a recordable criminal conviction. More significantly, the defendant may also risk losing his liberty, and therefore his livelihood. It is entirely appropriate that the more the defendant risks losing, the higher the standard of proof should be.

The reverse burden of proof

As is often the case with law, there are exceptions to the rule and there are limited circumstances where the standard of proof will be on the defendant to prove their defence. The most commonly used example the student of criminal law will encounter is the defence of diminished responsibility (see Chapter 6) where s 2(2) of the Homicide Act 1957 as amended by s 54(5) of the Coroners and Justice Act 2009, places the burden of proof on the defendant.

Thus, the standard of proof under normal circumstances is on the prosecution to prove the defendant's guilt beyond reasonable doubt, but if the defendant is required to prove a defence, the standard of proof is lowered to 'a balance of probability'.

THE PRACTICAL SIDE OF THE CRIMINAL LAW

From the outset, it is essential to use the correct terminology. Without a clear understanding, you will fall into poor habits that will remain with you throughout your studies.

The criminal law concerns the ability of the prosecution to prove the defendant's guilt. If the prosecution are unable to prove their case, the defendant's innocence is proved and he is acquitted.

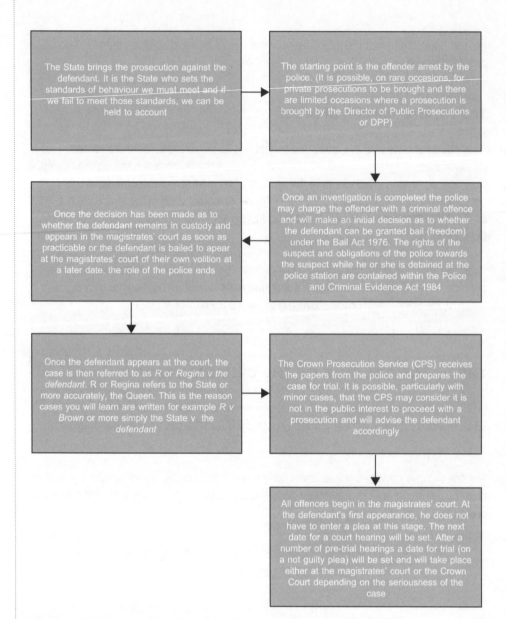

Figure 1.3 The process of a criminal offence from arrest to trial

THE CLASSIFICATION OF CRIMINAL OFFENCES

Criminal offences are classified by the level of seriousness of the offence with which the defendant is charged.

The most serious offences, such as murder, manslaughter, rape, robbery and wounding or causing grievous bodily harm with intent are referred to as *'indictable only'* offences and will be heard in the Crown Court where guilt or innocence will be determined by a jury. The judge in the Crown Court has the greatest powers of sentencing to reflect the seriousness of the offence.

There are a mid-range of offences which can be heard either in the magistrates' court (without a jury) or in the Crown Court (with a jury). These are referred to as *'either way offences'*. The type of offences which fall into this category include theft, burglary, wounding or inflicting grievous bodily harm (s 20 of the Offences Against the Person Act 1861). In order to decide where a case is to be heard, a *mode of trial* hearing takes place.

- If the magistrates feel their powers of sentencing are insufficient and the case is too serious to be heard in the magistrates' court, they will send (remit) the case to the Crown Court for trial.
- Even if the magistrates accept the case for trial in the magistrates' court, they can still remit the case to the Crown Court for sentence at the conclusion of the trial, if they consider their sentencing powers to be inadequate.
- If the magistrates accept the case for trial, the defendant then has a choice. He can either accept the magistrates' decision or he can decide to have his case heard in the Crown Court.
- What factors are relevant to the defendant's decision? Briefly, the defendant may choose to have his case tried by his peers rather than the magistrates on the basis that jury members may be more sympathetic to his defence rather than the magistrates who can be more 'case-hardened' (i.e. they have heard it all before!). However, the defendant must balance the decision against the potential of a harsher sentence if convicted in the Crown Court.

Since we have established that all cases begin in the magistrates' court, it follows that the magistrates' court is the more inferior of the courts. More serious cases (*either way offences* or *indictable only offences*) are heard by the Crown Court. If the defendant is tried in the magistrates' court, he may appeal against conviction and/or sentence to the Crown Court. On the other hand, if the defendant is tried in the Crown Court, he can still appeal against conviction and/or sentence, but now to the Court of Appeal (Criminal Division). It is not just the defendant who can appeal; the prosecution can and does appeal against sentence. Either party can appeal to the Supreme Court (or the House of Lords pre-2009). A party must have leave from the Court of Appeal to proceed to the Supreme Court, and this will only be granted if there is a question of great public importance involved. If the Court of Appeal refuses leave to appeal, an application can be made directly to the Supreme Court.

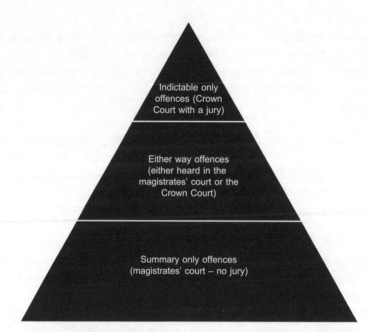

Figure 1.4 The classification of offences

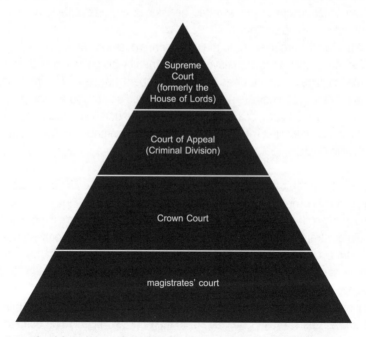

Figure 1.5 The hierarchy of criminal courts in England and Wales

THE CRIMINAL TRIAL

The UK has an adversarial system of trial which involves both parties presenting their case to the jury whose role it is to determine guilt or innocence. One disadvantage of this system is that the scales of justice do not appear equally balanced; this is because the State prosecutes and has resources and funding securely behind them. A defendant, in contrast, may be in receipt of legal funding (legal aid) if they cannot afford to fund their defence themselves or are receiving state benefits. There are, however, some minor cases where legal funding will be refused but the basic principle is where there is a risk of loss of livelihood, the defendant is likely to receive legal funding. It is the role of the judge to ensure that the trial is conducted fairly and properly. To this end, there are strict rules of evidence that must be adhered to and the prosecution must disclose all evidence they wish to rely on, together with all unused material, to the defence. The defence are not required to provide all the details about the defence, save for details of any alibi the defendant may wish to rely upon and the defence will also have disclosed any experts reports if relevant. As stated above, the defendant is cloaked in a presumption of innocence and it is at this time that the prosecution will seek to unravel it.

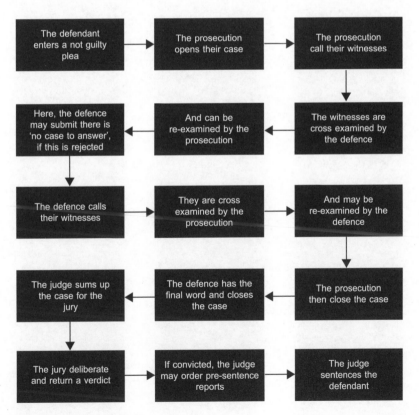

Figure 1.6 The trial process

FURTHER READING

It is important to appreciate the importance of reading the key cases. It is not sufficient to successfully study law by simply reading a summary of the case in any textbook. Any law student who wishes to achieve must read the cases in full.

Lord Bingham, 'A Criminal Code: Must we wait Forever?' [1999] Crim LR 694 – an insight into the crucial issue of whether the UK should have a criminal code.

In a law library or electronically, read the judgment of *R v Brown* and *R v Wilson*. Summarise the main principles of the judgment.

COMPANION WEBSITE

An online glossary compiled by the authors is available on the companion website: www.routledge.com/cw/beginningthelaw

Chapter 2
Actus reus, omissions and causation

LEARNING OBJECTIVES

By the end of the chapter, you should be able to:

- Demonstrate an understanding of the *actus reus* of a crime
- Appreciate the *actus reus* can also amount to an omission or a failure to act
- Understand the importance of establishing the causative link
- Demonstrate a clear understanding of the rules of causation

INTRODUCTION

There are two elements to a crime which are often referred to as the external and the internal elements: the **actus reus** and the **mens rea**. Both these terms are derived from the Latin phrase, '*Actus non facit reum nisi mens sit rea*', which means that a man is not liable for his acts alone, unless he acts with a guilty mind. In order to obtain a conviction against a defendant, the prosecution must be able to prove that the *actus reus* and *mens rea* elements are both present as well as proving the absence of a legally recognised **defence**.

In this chapter we will be considering the *actus reus* or the guilty act. We will look at how a **failure** or **omission to act can sometimes constitute an *actus reus***. We will also consider causation and the relationship between the act and the consequences of the act. *Mens rea* will be discussed in detail in Chapter 3.

Key Definition

The **actus reus** is the external element or the guilty act. The **mens rea** is the internal element or the guilty mind. Both are required to establish criminal liability.

ACTUS REUS

The *actus reus* (AR) is the physical element of the prohibited act. The term *AR* is fundamental to any criminal law course but it is potentially problematic. In *Miller* [1983] 2 AC 161, Lord Diplock was critical of the term *actus reus* as he said:

> it suggests that some positive act on the part of the accused is needed to make him guilty and that a failure or omission to act is insufficient to give rise to criminal liability.

Whilst the *AR* is more likely to be demonstrated in case law as a positive act, for example, the stabbing of the victim in a wounding case or the stealing of an item in theft, this essential element can also be an omission or a failure to act. The case of *Miller* is a good example (see page 24 for a more detailed discussion). Here, the defendant had created a dangerous situation and failed to take the necessary and appropriate steps to deal with it.

Every criminal offence must contain the *AR* – without it the defendant cannot be convicted. This is demonstrated in the case of *Deller* (1952) Cr App R 184 where the defendant wrongly believed he was deceiving the victim as to the rightful ownership of his car. As this was not in fact the case, the *actus reus* could not be proved, and the defendant could not be convicted.

Sources of the *actus reus*

For the *AR* to be proved the prosecution must be able to establish a prohibited act defined by either **common law** or **statute**.

Example

The definition of theft is contained in s 1 of the Theft Act 1968 as

> the dishonest appropriation of property belonging to another with the intention of permanently depriving the other of it.

What do you think the *AR* is? There is more than one element. Let's review it again, this time, with the *AR* elements underlined.

> the dishonest *appropriation* of *property belonging to another* with the intention of permanently depriving the other of it.

In this example, there is more than one *AR* element, the appropriation of property which belongs to another. As we will see in Chapter 9, all these elements have separate definitions but, for our purposes, the *AR* has three component parts, the '*appropriation*', '*property*' and '*belonging to another*'. If one part is not satisfied, the *AR* will not have been proved.

The *AR* and the *mens rea* (*MR*) must take place at the same time

If a conviction is to be obtained, the defendant must possess the necessary *MR* at the same time that the *AR* is committed.

This has caused certain difficulties, which are well illustrated in the case below.

KEY CASE: *Fagan v Metropolitan Police Commissioner* [1968] 3 All ER 442

Facts:

- The defendant was parking his car when he accidentally drove onto a policeman's foot.
- The policeman gesticulated to him to move his car, the defendant replied 'F**k off, you can wait'. He moved the car some 2 or 3 minutes later.
- He was convicted of the offence of assault but he appealed arguing that the *AR* and the *MR* were not committed at the same time.
- The assault was committed and the *AR* completed when he drove the car onto the policeman's foot, at this stage the defendant argued there was no *MR*, it was simply an accident.

Held:

The court dismissed his appeal explaining although his original act was unintentional, there came a point when he refused to move his car and at that point the *MR* was formed. Whilst it was not a criminal act at the beginning, it became a criminal act once he failed to move the car. Since the *MR* element was at that point deemed to be present and this was part of a continuing act or the same sequence of events, the defendant was convicted.

The *actus reus* must be voluntary

The *AR* of a crime must reflect a person's free will and autonomy and therefore must be voluntarily performed. A person could only be morally culpable if they have voluntarily committed an offence. If the person commits an offence involuntarily, and through no fault of their own, it would clearly be wrong to punish him for something over which he has no control.

External causes of involuntary behaviour or conduct

Example

If Adam, whilst travelling on a crowded train, suffers a muscle spasm in his leg, causing him to involuntarily kick Bertha, causing injury, he will not be liable for the assault as his act was involuntary. There is no *AR* and thus no criminal liability. Other similar examples could include a reflex action or an act committed whilst suffering from concussion.

In these circumstances the defendant may plead the defence of *automatism*.

Key Definition

Lord Denning in *Bratty v Attorney General of Northern Ireland* [1963] AC 386 defined automatism as 'an act which is done by the muscles without any control of the mind' and 'an act done by a person who is not conscious of what he is doing'.

However, for a defendant to successfully rely on the defence of automatism there must be a total lack of voluntary control. *Attorney General's Reference (No 2 of 1992)* [1993] 4 All ER 683 held that impaired, reduced or partial control is insufficient.

Internal causes of involuntary behaviour or conduct

In contrast to the above, if Chris, whilst sleepwalking, assaults Diane (*see Burgess* [1991] 2 All ER 769) this is considered to be conduct caused by an internal factor. In these circumstances Chris may plead the defence of *insanity or insane automatism*

The difficulty of this area is really demonstrated by the case of *Quick* [1973] QB 910 and led Lawton LJ to describe this area as 'a quagmire seldom entered nowadays save for those in desperate need of some sort of defence'.

The court had to consider the approach to diabetic defendants who commit offences whilst in either a hypoglycaemic state or a hyperglycaemic state. The former term, hypoglycaemia, refers to a low blood level due to an excess of insulin, as a result of which, the defendant could plead automatism as the excess insulin is an external factor. The latter term, hyperglycaemia, refers to a high blood sugar level due to a lack of insulin. Here the defendant could plead insanity because the conduct caused by the hyperglycaemia was an internal factor.

Exception to the principle that the *actus reus* must be voluntary

In very limited circumstances, the *AR* will refer to conduct or behaviour which is in itself voluntary but it is prohibited because of where the defendant is found or located. There is no specific *mens rea* for these offences, which are known as '**state of affairs' offences**.

KEY CASE: *Larsonneur* (1933) 24 Cr App Rep 74

Facts:

- A French woman was given leave to enter the UK subject to employment.
- She tried to marry, which would ensure her unrestricted leave in the UK but she was ordered to leave the UK and her passport was endorsed accordingly.
- She did not return to France but went to Ireland, an offence for which she was arrested and then deported back to the UK.
- On arrival in the UK she was charged and convicted of being an illegal alien in breach of the Aliens Order 1920, as leave to land in the UK had been refused.
- She appealed, arguing that landing in the UK was involuntary, as she had been deported and had no control over her destination.
- The *AR* therefore was not a voluntary act.

Held:

The court upheld her conviction – her mere presence in the UK was sufficient for the offence to have been committed. How she got there was largely irrelevant.

Similarly, in the case of *Winzar v Chief Constable of Kent, The Times*, 28 March 1983, a drunk was evicted from a hospital waiting area to the street by the police. He was then promptly arrested for being drunk on a public highway.

Both these cases illustrate similar principles, neither of the defendants had any control as to where they were, there was no voluntary act, but yet both of their convictions were upheld. Earlier, we referred to the elements of autonomy and free choice being a necessary element of the *AR*, but these rare examples prove an exception.

OMISSIONS OR FAILURES TO ACT

In most cases, it is straightforward to establish that the defendant's act can amount to a criminal offence. For example, if Edward stabs Freda, this would constitute a non fatal offence contrary to the Offences against the Persons Act 1861. However, if Freda was to die, Edward could be liable for murder or manslaughter. However, we will see that it is also possible for a defendant to have committed a criminal offence by an **omission or a failure to act**.

The general rule is that there is *no* criminal liability imposed upon a person for a failure to act. The jurist J.F. Stephen, *History of the Criminal Law of England* (1883) illustrates this principle with a classic example 'A sees B drowning and is able to save him by holding out his hand. A abstains from doing so in order that B may be drowned, and B is drowned. A has committed no offence.'

In order for A to be criminally liable for a failure or an omission to act, A must be under a duty of care. We could say that it is morally unacceptable not to intervene to help a person in distress – indeed, in other countries, such as France, a legal duty of acting as a 'Good Samaritan' is imposed. However, there is difficulty with this. Say for example, A decides to help rescue B but in doing so, breaks his leg. Does this amount to an assault? In criminal law, the defendant is likely to be liable. (There are also difficulties with causation which we will discuss later in this chapter.)

Can the law say with any certainty that but for A's failure to save B, B would not have drowned? If the prosecution could establish this beyond reasonable doubt, then even if A tried as hard as he could to rescue B but failed, his failure to rescue which leads directly to B's death (if proved) could lead to A's conviction! How could the prosecution prove this? What about the water's current, the depth, B's cooperation with being rescued, their relative strengths? The problems and difficulties that would be encountered in the prosecution attempting to prove their case are probably too numerous to mention. Even if we had an answer for every question, how do we know when to intervene? Where is the dividing line between the Good Samaritan and the nosy neighbour?

We can now consider some common law exceptions and some statutory exceptions to J.F. Stephen's general rule. If proved, the defendant will be liable for an omission or a failure to act.

Examples of some statutory exceptions

- s 6(4) of the Road Traffic Act 1988 – failing to provide a breath test when driving, or being in charge of a motor vehicle, under the influence of alcohol or after committing a traffic offence.
- s 19 of the Terrorism Act 2000 makes it an offence for a person who believes or suspects that another has committed an offence of terrorism or related act to fail to report that belief or suspicion to a constable.

Both the examples above demonstrate where the defendant's conduct constitutes a failure to act. Such failure amounts to a breach of statutory duty.

Common law exceptions

There are five categories of people, upon whom there is a positive duty to act.

- Where a special relationship exists between two parties, e.g. parent and child.
- Where the defendant voluntarily assumes responsibility of the victim, e.g. a relative or friend.
- Where the defendant, who holds a public office, is under a duty to act
- Where the defendant is under a contractual duty to act.
- Where the defendant has created a dangerous situation, he is under a duty to neutralise that danger.

Where a special relationship exists between two parties

Examples of special relationships between parties extend beyond parents and children to include, but not exclusively, teachers caring for children and medical professionals. It is from relationships within families where the most important common law derives.

The clear nature of the duty can be seen in *Gibbons v Proctor*.

KEY CASE: *Gibbons v Proctor* (1918) 13 Cr App R 134

Facts:

- A father and his partner were convicted of murdering his daughter by starving her to death.
- There was no familial relationship between his girlfriend and his daughter; but she had used his money to buy food for the house.
- She hit the child; the father knew this and failed to do anything to help the child.

Held:

They both owed a duty to care for her – the father because of their relationship and his girlfriend because of the nature of her relationship within the family unit.

Where the defendant voluntarily assumes care

In situations where the defendant has voluntarily assumed responsibility for the victim by for example, caring for them, a duty can be imposed upon them. Breach of this duty, (i.e. a failure or an omission to act) can result in criminal liability. In *Instan* [1893] 1 KB 450 Lord Coleridge CJ said 'It would not be correct to say that every moral obligation involves a legal duty; but every legal duty is founded upon a moral obligation.' The duty was both moral but also legal, as there was a form of contractual obligation in the sense that the money provided by the aunt for food was provided for both their benefits.

However, the case of *Stone and Dobinson* introduces new difficulties.

KEY CASE: *Stone and Dobinson* [1977] 2 All ER 341

Facts:

*   Mr Stone, a man of low intelligence, and partially deaf with very poor eyesight, lived with his partner, Dobinson, a younger woman who was described by the court as both ineffectual and inadequate.
*   Mr Stone's sister came to live with them. She suffered from anorexia and was partially reclusive.
*   They tried to care for her but were completely incapable of meeting even her most basic care needs.
*   She died in filth and squalor, and both the defendants were convicted of manslaughter.

Held:

They had failed to exercise their voluntarily assumed duty of care and their convictions were upheld on appeal.

The difficulty with this case is that it implies a subjective standard of care for those who voluntarily assume the care of another. Mr Stone took his sister into his home through sibling love. He had such complex difficulties himself that he had no hope of understanding her needs. Yet, he did the best he could, he tried to clean and bathe her. The reality appears to be that he did *his* subjective best which was clearly inadequate in the circumstances – if the law is imposing standards of care to be met, should Mr Stone have refused to care for his sister? The standard of care that Mr Stone offered was simply not good enough.

KEY CASE: *Airedale NHS Trust v Bland* [1993] 1 All ER

Facts:

- Anthony Bland was aged 21 when he suffered severe crushing injuries in the Hillsborough football stadium disaster.
- He remained in a PVS (persistent vegetative state).
- The doctors saw no hope of recovery and wished to cease treatment.
- The House of Lords had to consider whether a withdrawal or withholding of treatment was an omission and whether it was lawful.

Held:

Lord Mustill held that ending artificial nutrition and hydration by withdrawing the patient's feeding tube is an omission, not an act and it was not in the patient's best interests to continue treatment. It was therefore lawful to end treatment.

Anthony Bland's feeding tube was withdrawn and he died.

Where the defendant, who holds a public office is under a positive duty to act

In *Dytham* [1979] 3 All ER 641 a uniformed police officer failed to assist the victim who was being assaulted by bouncers outside a club. He failed to intervene or call an ambulance. He was convicted of misconduct of an officer of justice. His conviction was upheld on appeal as he neglected and omitted to perform his duty by assisting the victim.

Where the defendant is under a contractual duty to act

In *Pittwood* (1902) 19 TLR 37, a railway crossing keeper negligently left the crossing open. The victim was killed by a train. The defendant was convicted of manslaughter as he failed to perform his contractual duty to close the crossing gates.

Where the defendant has created a dangerous situation, he is under a duty to neutralise that danger

We have already referred to the case of *Miller* on page 16. The defendant was squatting, lit a cigarette and fell asleep. The mattress he was sleeping on caught fire. He woke up, moved rooms but failed to put the fire out. He was convicted of criminal damage contrary to s 1 and s 1(3) of the Criminal Damage Act 1971 (arson).

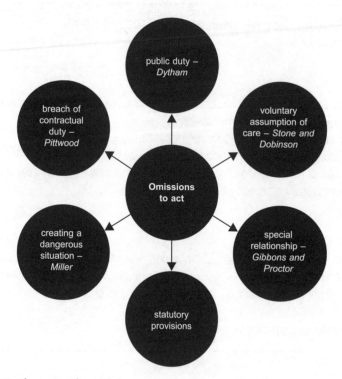

Figure 2.1 The ways in which an omission to act can be committed

CAUSATION

The prosecution must be able to prove a causative link between the prohibited act and the result. If the prosecution fails to prove the causative link, the defendant cannot be convicted.

This principle is illustrated in the case of *White* [1910] 2 KB 124. The defendant put cyanide in his mother's tea. He intended to poison and kill her, but she died of a heart attack before drinking the tea. Although he intended to kill her, his prohibited act (the poisoning) did not lead to her death. He could not be convicted of her murder.

On occasions, there may be more than one event that precedes the victim's injuries or death. The defendant may commit an unlawful act but there may be intervention by a third party that may break the chain of causation, absolving the defendant from liability. In reality, the courts are reluctant absolve the defendant from blame.

Establishing causation

There are **three rules** to be applied

- Would the result have occurred 'but for' the defendant's conduct? See *White* above.
- Were the defendant's actions more than a minimal, slight or trivial cause of the result? *Kimsey* [1996] Crim LR 35.
- Was there a new intervening act (a *novus actus interveniens*) that breaks the chain of causation between the defendant's actions and the result? This is most commonly relevant to medical treatment or to the victim's action or inaction.

The issue of causation is best understood as a two-stage process. It is necessary for the prosecution to prove that the defendant's actions are both a legal and a factual cause of the result.

Factual causation

Factual causation is usually established by the 'but for' test. We could ask 'but for' the defendant's actions would the prohibited consequences have occurred? In *White* (above), factual causation could not be proved as the defendant's act did not lead to the victim's death.

KEY CASE: *Pagett* (1983) 76 Cr App R 279

Facts:

- The defendant kidnapped his pregnant girlfriend and used her as a 'human shield' in an armed standoff with police.
- The defendant shot at the police who returned fire and shot the girlfriend who later died.
- The defendant was convicted of manslaughter and appealed against his conviction.

Held:

The Court of Appeal dismissed his appeal. Even though he did not kill his girlfriend himself, and therefore was not the sole or even the main cause of death, he contributed significantly to the act. Had he not been armed and used his girlfriend as a hostage, she would not have died.

Principle:

The defendant's 'act need not be the sole or even the main cause (of the result)', the defendant's act need only 'contribute significantly to that result' per Goff LJ.

Smith [1959] 2 QB 35 concerned a soldier who had stabbed the victim twice during a fight. Whilst the victim was on the stretcher he was dropped twice. He then received inappropriate treatment and failed to receive a much needed blood transfusion. He subsequently died and the defendant was convicted of his murder. He appealed, arguing that the acts subsequent to the stabbing broke the chain of causation and he could not be liable.

Lord Parker CJ held as follows;

> if at the time of death the original wound is still an operating cause and a substantial cause, then the death can properly be said to be the result of the wound, albeit that some other cause of death is also operating ... Putting it another way, only if the second cause is so overwhelming as to make the original wound merely part of the history can it be said that death does not flow from the wound.

There was no break in the chain of causation.

Medical treatment

The courts are reluctant to allow negligent or poor medical treatment to act as a *novus actus interveniens*.

Rarely, and most unusually, medical treatment in *Jordan* (1956) 40 Cr App R 152 was considered to be 'palpably wrong' and broke the chain of causation, exonerating the defendant.

KEY CASE: *Cheshire* [1991] 3 All ER 670

The court chose not to follow the principle established in *Jordan* and held that medical negligence is extremely unlikely to break the chain of causation.

Facts:

- The defendant shot the victim in the stomach.
- He was treated in hospital but subsequently died.
- Post mortem evidence confirmed negligent treatment led directly to the victim's death.
- The stab wounds received had largely healed at the time of the victim's death.

Held:

Beldam LJ stated that acts involving negligent medical treatment were all too common for it to be considered 'extraordinary'. The judge should direct the jury that the defendant's acts need not be the sole or even main cause of death, provided they contributed significantly to the result. He continued 'Even though negligence in the treatment of the victim was the immediate cause of death, the jury should not regard it as excluding the responsibility of the accused unless the negligent treatment was so independent of his acts, and in itself so potent in causing death, that they regard the contribution made by his acts as insignificant.'

Principle:

Even if the medical treatment is the actual cause of death, the courts are reluctant to exonerate the defendant from guilt unless the negligent treatment is so material that it renders the original wounds the defendant caused as insignificant.

On-the-spot question

? Malcolm is stabbed by Dwayne and is taken to hospital. On arrival at hospital, the Accident and Emergency doctor fails to notice that Malcolm is allergic to antibiotics. Unfortunately, he has just administered IV antibiotics. Malcolm dies. Is Dwayne liable for Malcolm's murder?

The victim's actions and potential breaks in the chain of causation

> **KEY CASE: *Blaue* [1975] 3 All ER 446 (The Thin Skull Rule)**
>
> Facts:
>
> - The defendant stabbed a woman who was taken to hospital.
> - She refused a life-saving blood transfusion as she was a Jehovah's Witness.
> - She died and the defendant was convicted of manslaughter.
> - He appealed on the grounds that her refusal was unreasonable and should break the chain of causation.
>
> Held:
>
> Lawton LJ held that 'It has long been the policy of the law that those who use violence on other people must take their victims as they find them. This, in our judgment, means the whole man, not just the physical man.'
>
> Principle:
>
> The **thin skull rule** applies; one must take one's victim as one finds them. This means that the defendant will be liable even if the victim suffers from a condition from which the defendant is not aware of, which makes him more susceptible to injury or even death. Thus, the defendant will not be exonerated from blame if the victim's condition is worsened through either an unforeseen physical or mental condition.

Escape cases

In some situations, the victim may attempt to escape from the defendant. If the victim injures herself in the course of an escape, can the defendant claim that the victim actions amounted to a *novus actus interveniens*? If the method of escape is reasonably foreseeable then it is unlikely to break the chain of causation. However, Stephenson LJ said obiter in *Roberts* [1971] that the chain of causation could be broken if the escape was so 'daft' or so 'unexpected . . . that . . . no reasonable man could be expected to foresee it'.

Drug dealing

Difficulty arises when considering the liability of a person who supplies drugs to another. If A supplies drugs to B and then prepares the syringe and ties the tourniquet around B's arm for B to inject himself, should A be liable if B subsequently dies?

Historically, the defendant drug supplier would not be liable as cases such as *Dalby and Armstrong* [1982] 1 All ER 916 held that the act of self injection was a voluntary act which broke the chain of causation. The law then became somewhat muddied until 2007.

In *Kennedy* (2007), the House of Lords returned the law to the accepted norm and after two unsuccessful appeals by the defendant held that where an adult makes an autonomous decision, exercising his own free will, the chain of causation will be broken and the defendant will not be guilty of his manslaughter where he supplied the drugs.

Self-test question

Andy is a drugs supplier. He prepares a syringe of heroin and passes it to Shane to inject. If Shane dies, will Andy be criminally liable?

Basic principles and omissions to act case law	Principle
Fagan (1968)	If the *AR* and the *MR* do not coincide, they will be considered to be part of a continuing act
Larsonneur (1933) *Winzar* (1983)	Rare exceptions to the rule that the *AR* must be voluntary
Gibbons and Proctor (1918)	Where a special relationship between parties exists, a failure to act can result in criminal liability
Stone and Dobinson (1977) *Instan* (1893)	Where one party voluntarily assumed care for the other a failure to act can result in criminal liability
Bland (1993)	Withdrawal of artificial feeding did not amount to an omission to act
Dytham (1979)	Public office imposed a duty to act
Pittwood (1902)	Contractual obligation imposed a duty to act
Miller (1983)	Where the defendant created a dangerous situation, there is an obligation to act to avoid it

Causation case law	Principles
White (1910)	Factual causation – but for test
Pagett (1983)	The defendant's act has to be a substantial and operating cause of death
Smith (1959)	The chain of causation will not be broken even if there is another cause of death unless the second wound is so overwhelming as to make the first wound part of history
Jordan (1956)	Rarely, medical treatment that was 'palpably wrong' broke the chain of causation
Cheshire (1991)	The defendant's acts need not be the sole or even main cause of death, provided they contributed significantly to the result. The chain of causation will not be broken
Blaue (1975)	The defendant must take the victim as he finds him
Roberts (1971)	An escape that was so 'daft' that no reasonable person would undertake could break the chain of causation
Kennedy (2007)	A drug supplier will not be liable if the victim self injects. The chain of causation will be broken

SUMMARY

- The *AR* must be proved by the prosecution and is usually a voluntary positive act.
- An *AR* can be committed by an omission or a failure to act.
- A causative link must be proved by the prosecution.
- The *AR* must cause the prohibited consequences.
- There are rare occasions where causation is broken, exonerating the defendant of blame.

ISSUES TO THINK ABOUT FURTHER

Do you agree with the decision of *Kennedy*? If a drug supplier provides drugs to another, should he be criminally liable even if he has no role in the injecting of the drugs? Why do you think the courts came to this decision? You may find it useful to read the full judgment. It is lengthy but the judgment discusses all previous relevant case law. Reading cases in full will provide you with the level of understanding you will need for your studies. Getting into good habits early in your study of the law is very beneficial.

FURTHER READING

Ashworth, A, 'The scope of criminal liability for omissions' (1989) 105 LQR 424 – for a discussion of the criminal liability in relation to omissions to act.

Williams, G, 'Criminal omissions – the conventional view' (1991) 107 LQR 87 – a further article discussing liability for omissions or failures to act.

Elliot, C and De Than, C, 'Prosecuting the drug dealer when a drug user dies: R v Kennedy (No.2)' (2006) 69 Modern Law Review 986 – an analysis of the seminal case of *Kennedy* and the law relating to the criminal accountability of drug dealers.

COMPANION WEBSITE

An online glossary compiled by the authors is available on the companion website: www.routledge.com/cw/beginningthelaw

Chapter 3
Mens rea

LEARNING OBJECTIVES

By the end of the chapter, you should be able to:

- Demonstrate an understanding of the *mens rea* of a crime
- Appreciate the test to be applied to determine intention
- Understand the current legal test or recklessness
- Demonstrate a knowledge of the background of the law as it stands today
- Appreciate what amounts to a strict liability offence and understand the strict liability role offences play in the criminal law

INTRODUCTION

In Chapter 1 we referred to two elements of a crime, the **actus reus** and the **mens rea** which originate from the Latin phrase, *'Actus non facit reum nisi mens sit rea'*. The principle explains that a man is not liable for his acts alone, unless he acts with a guilty mind. In this chapter we consider in more detail the *mens rea* or the 'guilty mind'.

It is for the prosecution to prove the *mens rea* of the offence the defendant is charged with. If the prosecution is unable to prove the *mens rea*, the defendant cannot be liable for the offence. The only offences where the prosecution need not prove the *mens rea*, as we shall see, are offences of strict liability.

> ### Example
>
> For ease of understanding, it might be useful to demonstrate the *mens rea* of an offence as an example. Within s 1 of the Theft Act 1968, the *mens rea* is the *dishonest intention* to permanently deprive. Hence, the prosecution must prove both the element of *dishonesty* and the element of *intention*.

There are different forms of *mens rea*, the most culpable being intention and the least culpable strict liability. It follows that those who commit offences with intention are naturally more morally blameworthy than those who commit offences negligently. Negligence as such is not a form of *mens rea* as it refers to a standard of behaviour or conduct which falls below that which a reasonable man would ordinarily expect, rather than a specific state of mind. We therefore only consider negligence briefly in this chapter.

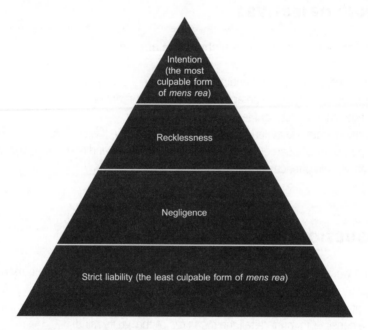

Figure 3.1 Diagram illustrating forms of *mens rea*

INTENTION

Criminal offences which require *intention* as its *mens rea* are often the most serious offences. For example, where the offence of murder is concerned, the prosecution must be able to prove the defendant *intended* to kill or cause grievous bodily harm. Where a person intends to commit a serious offence, the sentencing is often more severe, for example, a mandatory life sentence for murder. This makes perfect sense. If Tom intends to murder Steven, he should be prepared for the consequences when he is sentenced!

The word 'intention' in normal everyday usage causes the reader no difficulties but 'intention' in the criminal law has been notoriously ambiguous, lacking in clarity and often redefined by the courts. It is essential that any term in criminal law is clear, transparent and unambiguous so the defendant clearly understands and appreciates the consequences of his actions and the extent of his liability.

The historical development of the meaning of 'intention'

In *Hyam* [1975] 1 AC 55, the defendant poured petrol through the letter box of her former partner's fiancée's home. She had not intended to kill the two children that died in the fire that followed. However, she was convicted of murder as it was held that intention could be established if the defendant appreciated that death or serious harm was *highly probable*. It took another 10 years before the courts had an opportunity to redefine intention in *Moloney* [1985] 1 AC 905. Here, the defendant and his stepfather were engaged in a game of 'fastest draw' with the defendant's shotgun when he accidentally killed his stepfather. Although he was convicted of murder at first instance, he successfully appealed on the basis that intention could only be satisfied by establishing the defendant *foresaw* death or serious harm was *a natural consequence of the defendant's act.* Since the defendant could not foresee the accident, his conviction of murder was substituted for manslaughter. In less than a year, the issue of intention was once more before the courts. *Hancock and Shankland* [1986] AC 455 concerned two striking miners who had pushed a concrete block from a railway bridge onto the motorway. They had not intended murder or serious harm, they had only intended to block the motorway. The court convicted the two miners of murder on the basis that the greater probability of a consequence occurring, the more it must have been foreseen, and thus the greater the probability the consequences must have been intended.

KEY CASE: *R v Nedrick* [1986] 1 WLR 1025

Facts:

- Similar to the facts in *Hyam*, the defendant poured paraffin through a woman's letterbox in order to frighten her.
- He set the paraffin alight and the fire killed her child.
- The defendant maintained he only wanted to frighten her, not to harm her or her child but was convicted of murder and appealed.

Held:

The Court of Appeal rejected the test in earlier cases and Lord Lane CJ said as follows: 'The jury should be directed they are not entitled to infer the necessary intention, unless they feel sure that death or serious bodily harm was a virtual certainty (barring some unforeseen intervention) as a result of the defendant's action and the defendant appreciated that such was the case.'

The law as it stands today

Thus, *Nedrick* represents a move from defining intention through degrees of probability to one of virtual certainty.

On-the-spot question

 Sam pushes Edna off a bridge into fast flowing deep water below. He knows she is unable to swim. Edna drowns. Sam is charged with murder. Is he likely to be convicted of murder?

Apply the test in *Nedrick* above. When Sam pushes Edna off the bridge, you may conclude that death or grievous bodily harm was a virtual certainty. *You* can conclude this as if you were a member of the jury as it is an objective test. It is therefore for the jury to determine, on the facts as they present themselves, whether death or grievous bodily harm would be a virtual certainty. The second part of the test is that the defendant must have been aware that such was the case. In this example, Sam knew that Edna could not swim and the subjective part of this test is easily satisfied. In this example, the jury can infer intention, the requisite *mens rea* for the intention of murder.

The case of *Woollin* approved the test in *Nedrick*.

KEY CASE: *Woollin* [1999] 1 AC 82

Facts:

- The defendant lost his temper when his four-month-old baby began to cry.
- After shaking the baby, he threw him across the room where he hit a wall and died.
- The defendant maintained he did not intend to kill or cause grievous bodily harm.

Held:

The trial judge summed up using the term 'substantial risk' which was clearly a misdirection as it once more confused intention with recklessness. The defendant appealed and a verdict of manslaughter was substituted.

The House of Lords court approved the direction in the case of *Nedrick* save for one aspect. The court changed the word 'infer' to the word 'find'.

Summary of the current law

As a result of the cases of *Nedrick* and *Woollin* we can say: if the jury, having heard the evidence feel sure that death or grievous bodily harm was a virtual certain result of the defendant's actions AND the defendant appreciated as much, the jury are entitled to *find* that the defendant has the intention for murder.

RECKLESSNESS

The *mens rea* referred to as recklessness can be defined as where the defendant takes an unjustified risk. A defendant who is reckless is considered to be less criminally culpable or blameworthy because recklessness requires a lack of foresight of the consequences as opposed to knowledge of a consequence being virtually certain.

> **Example**
>
> Compare the two scenarios:
>
> Aki steals Paulina's laptop as he wishes to keep it for himself – here he intends to deprive Paulina of her possession – this involves a high degree of criminal culpability.
>
> Aki drives Paulina's car extremely fast. He explains he is very familiar with the roads but crashes and Paulina is badly hurt. Aki does not intend to hurt Paulina but the unjustified risk he takes results in her injuries. Although you may consider this example more serious because of the consequences, Aki is less morally culpable because he did not intend the consequences and simply acted unreasonably or unjustifiably.

The historical development of the meaning of 'recklessness'

Historically, whether the defendant was reckless was tested by the application of a subjective test.

KEY CASE: *Cunningham* [1957] 2 QB 396

Facts:

- The defendant broke a gas pipe to obtain money from a gas meter.
- The broken pipe allowed gas to seep through to the adjoining house causing injury to a neighbour.
- The defendant was charged with maliciously causing another to take a noxious thing so as to endanger life, an offence under s 23 of the Offences Against the Person Act 1861.

Held:

The judge directed that the term 'maliciously' meant 'wickedly'. The defendant appealed against conviction. The court applied a subjective test of the term recklessness.

In order for the defendant to be convicted, it was necessary for the prosecution to prove that the defendant foresaw harm would occur, but went on to take the risk nonetheless.

In this case the prosecution would have to prove that the defendant foresaw the risk of the escape of gas seeping through the wall, causing injury to the neighbour AND went on to take that risk.

The leading case of *Cunningham* was subsequently applied in the case of *Stephenson* [1979] 1 QB 695 where the defendant, a paranoid schizophrenic, climbed into a haystack and then set fire to it in order to keep warm. He was charged with arson contrary to the Criminal Damage Act 1971. The lower courts applied an objective test holding that the defendant would be guilty if a reasonable person would realise that such a risk would occur. However, the Court of Appeal quashed his conviction by applying the subjective test set down in *Cunningham*. It was necessary for the jury to decide what *this* particular defendant foresaw and here, due to his condition, the defendant did not foresee the risk.

However, the test to be applied to recklessness changed to an objective test in the case of *Caldwell*.

KEY CASE: *Caldwell* [1982] AC 341

Facts:

- The defendant, whilst drunk, set fire to a hotel following a dispute with the owner.
- He was charged with arson and argued that he was so intoxicated he gave no thought as to whether his act would create a risk of injury.

Held:

Although this case was concerned with the issue of intoxication (which is no defence to a charge of criminal damage), the House of Lords took the opportunity to reconsider recklessness.

Key Definition

A person would be guilty if he does an act that would create an obvious risk of damage AND when he carries out that act, he gives no thought to the risk of any damage OR recognises the risk and carries on with the act nonetheless.

Objective recklessness remained the test for recklessness for several years. The test was, however, subject to criticism for its harshness. No case illustrates this more than the case of *Elliot v C* [1983] 1 WLR 939. C was a 14-year-old girl with low intelligence. She took refuge in a shed and poured white spirit onto the floor and lit the accelerant causing a fire. She was charged with criminal damage contrary to ss 1 and 3 of the Criminal Damage Act 1971. At first instance she was acquitted as the court accepted that she lacked the understanding and maturity of age to appreciate the risk of damage. The Crown's appeal was upheld on the basis that a subjective test was not appropriate and that an objective test was to be applied. C was convicted on the basis that the ordinary person (which C clearly was not) would have appreciated the risk of setting white spirit alight.

The objective test of recklessness remained the law until the case of *R v Gemmell and Richards*.

KEY CASE: *R v Gemmell and Richards* [2003] UKHL 50

Facts:

- The defendants were young boys of 11 and 12 years of age playing behind a shop.
- They set fire to some newspapers and threw them under a wheelie bin.
- The bin caught fire and spread, causing £1 million of damage.
- The boys argued they expected the newspapers to simply burn out and did not appreciate the risk of the fire spreading in the way it did and causing the extensive damage.

Held:

At first instance, the jury, bound by the application of the objective nature of *Caldwell* found the defendants guilty. The conviction was based on the argument that the risk of damage would have been obvious to a reasonable man.

On appeal to the House of Lords, the objective test in *Caldwell* was overruled and the law reverted to the pre-*Caldwell* position of *Cunningham*.

In reverting to a subjective test in *Cunningham*, the court applied the test which was proposed by the Law Commission and set out in clause 18(c) of the Criminal Code Bill 1989.

The House of Lords held that a person is said to act recklessly within the meaning of s 1 of the Criminal Damage Act 1971 with respect to

(i)   a circumstance when he is aware of a risk that exists or will exist;
(ii)   a result when he is aware of a risk; that it will occur; and it is, in the circumstances known to him unreasonable to take that risk.

Lord Steyn described departing from *Caldwell* as *'irresistible'* and Lord Bingham gave four reasons for overruling *Caldwell*.

- For a defendant to be liable for a serious offence there should be evidence not just of an act (or omission) the defendant caused but also that his state of mind was culpable. Whilst it is clearly blameworthy to take an obvious and significant risk of causing injury to another person, it is not as clearly blameworthy to do something that involves risking an injury to another if that person does not perceive the risk. Reckless acts should not submit a person to conviction of a serious offence.

- The *Caldwell* test is *'capable of leading to obvious unfairness'*. Here, the jury felt it *'neither moral not just'* to convict a defendant (in this case a child) on the basis of what someone else may have appreciated, when the defendant in fact has no appreciation himself.
- Criticism of the decision in *Caldwell* should not be ignored where such criticism is widespread amongst academics, the judiciary and practitioners.
- There was a 'misinterpretation' of the term 'reckless' which was 'apt to cause injustice'. Thus it was necessary to correct the misinterpretation.

Recklessness today

The test for the *mens rea* of recklessness is a subjective one. However, whether or not it is reasonable for the defendant to take the risk which he is aware of is a question for the jury to decide.

NEGLIGENCE

Negligence is conduct or behaviour that falls below the standard to be expected of the reasonable man, thus it is objectively tested. One usually encounters negligence in the civil law and there is justifiably a question as to whether negligence can correctly be used to describe a form of *mens rea* in order to incur criminal liability.

Negligence is, however, relevant to some statutory offences where it forms the basis of many driving offences. For example, s 3 of the Road Traffic Act 1988 where negligence forms the basis of the offence of driving without due care and attention, an offence which is objectively judged – that is, according to the standard of the reasonable man. Negligence is also essential to the offence of gross negligence manslaughter, which we consider in Chapter 5.

THE COINCIDENCE OF *ACTUS REUS* AND *MENS REA*

In Chapter 1 we saw that in order to be convicted of a criminal offence the defendant must possess the *mens rea* and the *actus reus* of an offence, but no mention was made as to whether these two elements must be committed at the same time.

Example

A hits B, causing injury to B. He has been reckless as to whether injury will be caused and recklessness satisfies the *mens rea* for common assault, assault occasioning actual bodily harm contrary to s 47 of the Offences Against the Person Act 1861 and grievous bodily harm contrary to s 20 of the OAPA. The *mens rea* of assault occurs at a point during the *actus reus* and no difficulty arises.

'Coincidence of *actus reus* and *mens rea*' merely questions whether the defendant can still be convicted if the *actus reus* and the *mens rea* do not occur at the same moment in time. The answer to the question is that the defendant can indeed still be convicted and the problem of a lack of coincidence between the *actus reus* and the *mens rea* was illustrated in *Fagan v Metropolitan Police Commissioner* [1969] 1 QB 439 in Chapter 2. We saw that whilst there was no coincidence of the *mens rea* and the *actus reus*, the court upheld the defendant's conviction on the basis that the *mens rea* and the *actus reus* were part of the same continuing act. The difficulties of a lack of coincidence in the *mens rea* and *actus reus* were further shown in the following case, where the court treated the *mens rea* of the offence and the *actus reus*, which were separate in time, as one continuing event.

KEY CASE: *Thabo Meli v R* [1954] 1 WLR 288

Facts:

- The defendant hit the victim and thought he had killed him.
- He then pushed the body over a cliff.
- The defendant did not die until he landed at the bottom of the cliff.
  The defendant was convicted, but appealed arguing that whilst he may have had *mens rea* at the time he hit him, he did not have *mens rea* at the time he pushed him over the cliff, the act which killed the victim, because he believed he was already dead.

Held:

The court upheld the defendant's appeal on the basis that all the events could not be distinguished and according to Lord Reid were 'impossible to divide up what was really one series of acts'.

THE DOCTRINE OF TRANSFERRED MALICE

Example

Derek intends to cause injury to Edwardo. He lashes out at him with a knife but he accidentally trips and stabs Fransisco instead. He may have committed the *actus reus* of grievous bodily harm but he had no *mens rea* to stab Fransisco, indeed, Derek may not have even known that Fransisco was standing there. However, the law would be inadequate if it did not hold Derek accountable for his actions. It would hardly be morally sustainable if Derek did not face criminal charges due to his incompetence of failing to stab Edwardo. How can Derek be convicted of a criminal offence? In these circumstances, the law permits the *mens rea* to be transferred from Edwardo whom he intended to injure to Fransisco whom he subsequently injured.

KEY CASE: *Latimer* (1886) 17 QBD 359

Facts:

- The defendant struck a man with a belt.
- The belt rebounded and hit the victim, causing a wound to her face.

Held:

The defendant's conviction was upheld on the basis that the defendant had set out to cause another injury with 'unlawful and malicious intent' and was 'guilty of what the law deems malice against the person injured, because the offender is doing an unlawful act, and has that which the judges call general malice'.

However, *Latimer* distinguished the earlier case of *Pembliton* (1874) 2 CCR 119, where the defendant threw a stone at some people he had been fighting with. The stone missed, breaking a window. In these circumstances his conviction for unlawfully and maliciously causing damage to the window was quashed because although he had intended to injure a person with a stone, he had not intended to cause damage to a window. Nevertheless, the *mens rea* referred to here is 'intention'. It is perfectly possible that the defendant could be reckless, if he foresaw a risk of damage, and then continued by taking an unjustifiable risk.

In contrast, the case of *Attorney General's Reference (No 3 of 1994)* held that the doctrine of transferred malice did not extend to a double transfer.

KEY CASE: *Attorney General's Reference (No 3 of 1994)* **[1998] AC 245**

Facts:

- The defendant stabbed his girlfriend in the face, back and abdomen with a long-bladed kitchen knife.
- His girlfriend was pregnant and prematurely gave birth to a baby which died four months later.
- The defendant pleaded guilty to grievous bodily harm caused to his girlfriend and was then charged with murder subsequent to the baby's death.

Held:

The defendant's acquittal was upheld. The foetus was a separate organism from the mother and the defendant had no intention to kill or do serious harm to any person apart from the mother. The intention to stab the mother (who was alive), could not be transferred to an organism (who was not alive), which in turn could not be the victim of murder.

Furthermore, the court rejected the concept of double transferred intent; that is, once from the mother to the foetus and then from the foetus to the baby that was subsequently born.

STRICT LIABILITY

Where offences of strict liability are concerned, the *mens rea* need not be proven in relation to at least one aspect of the *actus reus* but may have to be proved for some other element of the *actus reus*. Thus, it is perfectly possible for the prosecution to prove their case without evidence of any *mens rea* at all and the defendant can be convicted in the absence of proof of fault.

To summarise, it appears possible, on face value, for the defendant to be convicted without proving intention, recklessness or negligence, or even that the defendant was at fault in some way (which is entirely contrary to what you have learnt about the need for *mens rea*). Strict liability offences are often set down by statute (Acts of Parliament).

One may suppose that the *mens rea* of an offence is automatically contained within statute, and more often it is, illustrated by words such as' intention' and recklessness, but sometimes statutes are silent as to *mens rea*. What happens on these occasions? It is then a matter of judicial reasoning to consider whether statutory interpretation can assist by considering Parliament's intention at the time the statute was enacted, or by looking at previously decided cases to help determine how to consider the case before them. The case of *Gammon (Hong Kong) v Attorney General of Hong Kong* illustrates just this situation.

KEY CASE: *Gammon (Hong Kong) v Attorney General of Hong Kong* **[1985] AC 1**

Facts:

- The defendants were involved in constructing a building in Hong Kong which collapsed.
- They were charged with deviating from the plans in a material way likely to cause injury.
- There was no evidence that the defendants knew the deviation was material.

Held:

In the lower courts the defendants were convicted and they appealed. Lord Scarman dismissed the appeal and set out the test to be applied in order to determine whether an offence is one of strict liability.

The strict liability test

1. There is a presumption that *mens rea* is required before a person can be found guilty of a criminal offence.
2. The presumption is stronger where the case is 'truly criminal'.
3. The presumption applies to statutory offences and can be displaced but only if the *mens rea* is clearly stated in the statute or implied from the statute.
4. If the statute is of social concern or public safety, the presumption can be displaced.
5. Even in cases concerning the above, the presumption of *mens rea* will apply unless the existence of strict liability will promote the objectives of the Act in ensuring greater vigilance to prevent the prohibited act.

In *Gammon* the court held the offence was one of strict liability as the statute existed to ensure that public safety standards were upheld.

If we consider each of the points above individually, we can see their application. The presumption of *mens rea* referred above was confirmed in the case of *Sweet v Parsley* [1970] AC 132, where the defendant, a school teacher, sublet a house to students but was unaware the tenants smoked cannabis. She was charged with being involved in the management of premises used for the purposes of smoking cannabis where the statute was silent as to *mens rea*. Lord Reid said in these circumstances 'whenever a section is silent as to *mens rea* there is a presumption that, in order to give effect to the will of Parliament, we must read in words appropriate to require *mens rea*'.

Similarly, in the case of *B (a minor) v DPP* [2000] 2 AC 428, a 15-year-old boy asked a younger girl to perform oral sex on him and was charged with inciting a child under the age of 14 to commit acts of gross indecency. Although he was convicted at first instance his appeal was allowed and the House of Lords held that his state of mind was relevant. Here, he honestly believed she was over the age of 14. Even though the Act, under which he was charged, was silent as to the *mens rea*, the need for a state of mind was read into it.

It is the case that there is a presumption of *mens rea* where the case is 'truly criminal' as shown in both the cases above and where, if convicted, a custodial sentence could be imposed by the courts. It is therefore satisfactory that strict liability cases tend to be regulatory offences, where the breach tends to be punished by a financial penalty. Strict liability can concern issues such as social concern over the abuse in alcohol as in *Cundy v Le Cocq* (1884) 13 QBD 207, or prevention of pollution as in *Alphacell v Woodward* [1972] AC 824, where the existence of *mens rea* was not relevant to the appeal of a company charged with permitting matter to pollute a river. Perhaps the offence of drink driving contrary to s 5 of the Road Traffic Act 1988 is a more commonly known offence of strict liability.

SUMMARY

- The prosecution must, in almost all circumstances, with the exception of some strict liability offences, prove the defendants state of mind.
- The more serious the offence, the more likely it is, that intention is the required state of mind.
- The current test of intention is the 'virtual certainty' test.
- Recklessness or inadvertent risk taking is a suitable form of *mens rea* for less serious offences, where less moral culpability is attached.
- The current test of recklessness is largely subjective.

Table 3.1 Cases concerning the definition of 'intention'

Case	Principle
Hyam (1975)	Intention would be satisfied if the defendant knew death or serious harm was highly probable
Moloney (1985)	Intention would be satisfied if the defendant foresaw death or serious harm as a natural consequence of the defendant's act
Hancock and Shankland (1986)	The greater the probability of a consequence occurring, the more it must have been foreseen and therefore the greater the probability it must have been intended
Nedrick (1986)	Intention can be inferred if death or serious bodily harm was a virtual certainty of the defendant's action and the defendant appreciated that such was the case
Woollin (1999)	Confirmed the test in *Nedrick*. 'Infer' became 'find'

Table 3.2 Cases concerning the definition of 'recklessness'

Case	Principle
Cunningham (1957)	Recklessness subjectively tested
Stephenson (1979)	Confirmed recklessness was a subjective test
Caldwell (1982)	Test now became objective
Elliot v C (1983)	Harshness of test shown
R v Gemmell and Richards (2003)	Test reverts to subjective

ISSUES TO THINK ABOUT FURTHER

To what extent do you consider the subjective test in recklessness is correct? When considering your answer, try to use case law to support your opinion. This is an essential skill to develop and as always, good habits should be developed as early as possible!

FURTHER READING

Ensure you read the key cases in full – try and ensure you can extract the legal principles from them.

Norrie, A, 'After Woollin' [1999] Crim LR 582 – a thorough and reflective article on intention.

Reid, K, 'Strict Liability; Some Principles for Parliament' (2008) 29(3) Statute Law Review 173–94 – a lengthy but detailed and helpful article on the complexity of strict liability offences.

COMPANION WEBSITE

An online glossary compiled by the authors is available on the companion website: www.routledge.com/cw/beginningthelaw

Chapter 4
Murder and involuntary manslaughter

LEARNING OBJECTIVES

By the end of the chapter you should be able to:

- Understand the common law definition of murder
- Be able to demonstrate a thorough understanding of the elements of the *actus reus* of murder
- Understand the offence of unlawful act manslaughter and be able to clearly explain the elements
- Demonstrate an understanding of gross negligence manslaughter and its component parts

INTRODUCTION

Text books often refer to the term 'homicide'. This simply refers to the killing of another person but it is a term that covers killings that are both lawful (self defence can justify a killing where reasonable force is used) and unlawful. Unlawful killing can refer to a range of offences, from murder (the most serious) to less serious offences, such as manslaughter. In turn, manslaughter can be described as voluntary or involuntary as the diagram below shows.

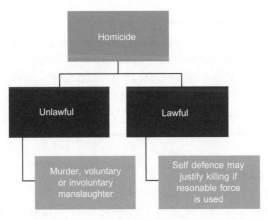

Figure 4.1 Diagram showing lawful and unlawful killing

Involuntary manslaughter includes unlawful act manslaughter and gross negligence manslaughter, whilst reckless and corporate manslaughter are newer offences.

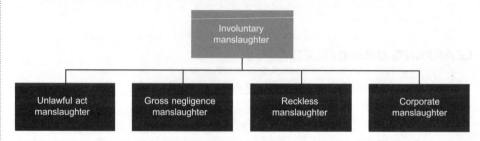

Figure 4.2 Diagram showing breakdown of involuntary manslaughter

THE OFFENCE OF MURDER

Murder is probably the most serious offence in the criminal justice system and, unusually, a common law offence. Its seriousness is reflected in sentencing as conviction will result in a mandatory life sentence. The sentencing judge will also set a 'tariff' – the minimum number of years the defendant will serve before he is eligible for parole. In contrast, with manslaughter the life sentence is discretionary. Of course, the defendant may be sentenced to life, but the judge has a wider range of sentences at his disposal.

Murder → common law offence → mandatory life sentence on conviction.

Manslaughter → common law offence → discretionary sentencing on conviction.

Key Definition

Sir Edward Coke, the jurist, classically defined murder (Coke 3 Inst. 47) as: 'Murder is when a man of sound memory, and of the age of discretion, unlawfully killeth within any country of the realm any reasonable creature in rerum natura under the King's peace, with malice aforethought, either expressly or implied by law (so as the party wounded, or hurt, etc. die of the wound or hurt etc within a year and a day of the same).'

The *mens rea* of murder

The *mens rea* of murder as defined by Coke is 'malice aforethought'. This is misleading as neither 'malice' nor 'aforethought' is required. The case of *Vickers* [1957] 2 QB 664 confirms that the accepted modern day definition of *mens rea* is the intention to kill or cause grievous bodily harm. Intention is proved by the application of the test of 'virtual certainty' as established in the cases of *Nedrick* and *Woollin* (see Chapter 3).

The *actus reus* of murder

From Coke's definition above we can extract four different elements of the *actus reus*:

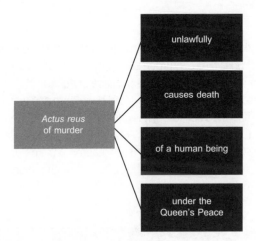

Figure 4.3 The elements of the *actus reus* of murder

What does 'unlawfully' mean?

Not all killings are unlawful. For example, killing during lawful military action is 'lawful.' Furthermore, the justificatory defence of self defence renders a killing lawful in circumstances which would otherwise be murder.

The defence of necessity was relevant in *Re A (Minors) Conjoined Twins: Medical Treatment)* [2000] 4 All ER 961. Doctors separated conjoined twins, Jodie and Mary, knowing that in doing so the weaker twin would die. Whilst the separation would be likely to satisfy the *mens rea* of murder, it would lack logic if doctors would be liable in these circumstances. Hence the court considered that the necessity (preserving the life of Jodie) would act as an appropriate defence.

On-the-spot question

?
Anthony and Bert are conjoined twins. A decision has been made to separate them. Bert is reliant upon the supply of blood from Adam's heart to his body. If the twins are separated, Bert will die. Explain why the doctors will not be liable for Bert's murder when it is virtually certain that Bert will die as a direct result of the operation.

What does 'causes death' mean?

We considered causation in detail in Chapter 2. The prosecution must prove beyond all reasonable doubt that the defendant is both the factual and the legal cause of the victim's death. If the prosecution are unable to prove both these elements, the defendant cannot be convicted of the victim's death.

What is 'a human being'?

When does life begin?
In order for the defendant to be convicted, the victim must be '*a reasonable creature in rerum natura*'. It is not possible to 'murder' an animal, but what is a 'reasonable creature'? The answer can be found in case law as the old case of *Poulton* (1832) 5 C & P 329 held a foetus was not a 'reasonable creature' until it had been born and was entirely independent from its mother's womb. Once delivered, it is capable of being murdered, even if the umbilical cord has not yet been cut (*Reeves* (1829) 9 C & P 25). In *Attorney-General's Reference (No 3 of 1994)* [1997] 3 All ER 936 (see Chapter 3) the defendant was acquitted of murder as he had no intention to harm the baby, even though the baby died some time after he stabbed the mother.

Example

The victim's injuries are caused by the defendant. The victim's injuries are serious and he is put on a life support machine. If the life support machine is subsequently switched off by doctor treating the patient, who is liable for the victim's death? Does switching off the life support machine amount to a *novus actus interveniens* so as to break the chain of causation and exonerate the defendant of guilt?

The House of Lords in *Airedale NHS Trust v Bland* [1993] AC 789 (see page 23) held that the act of switching of the life support machine is an omission to act rather than a positive act and therefore the doctor would not be criminally liable for murder. Equally, the act of switching off the life support machine and ending the victim's life would not amount to a break in the chain of causation.

When does life end?
Death is not defined by law but the accepted definition of death in the UK is the point at which brain stem death occurs. A patient on a life support system is still a reasonable creature and hence is capable of being murdered *Malcherek and Steel* [1981] 2 All ER 422.

The year and a day rule

The requirement that the victim dies '*within a year and a day*' was abolished by the Law Reform (Year and a Day Rule) Act 1996. As considerable advances had been made in the field of medical technology, patients are capable of being kept alive artificially for longer periods of time. It would be illogical if the defendant was unable to be convicted for murder simply because the victim was able to be sustained artificially. However, if the death occurs more than three years after the fateful act or omission, the consent of the Attorney General must be sought before a charge of murder can be brought.

UNLAWFUL ACT MANSLAUGHTER

Introduction

Unlawful act manslaughter is an unlawful homicide committed without '*malice aforethought*'. Here, the defendant carries out an intentional unlawful criminal act. There is no 'intention' to cause physical harm but the act results in the victim's death. It has often been considered to be controversial because a defendant can be convicted of unlawful act manslaughter even though he may not have foreseen any risk of harm in his act. However, he has engaged in an unlawful criminal act and must be held liable if the victim dies as a result, even if those consequences are entirely unforeseen.

KEY CASE: *R v Larkin* [1943] 1 All ER 217

Facts:

- The defendant found his girlfriend drinking with another man at a party.
- The defendant brandished a sharp razor and threatened the other man.
- Under the influence of drink, the victim fell on the razor, accidentally cutting her throat. She died as a result.

Held:

The defendant was convicted of unlawful act manslaughter.

The court confirmed the following elements must be established for unlawful act manslaughter to be proven:

- The act must be an intentional act.
- The act must be unlawful.
- The act must be objectively dangerous.
- The act must cause death.

In *Larkin*, the defendant intentionally waved a sharp razor at another, in itself an unlawful act and clearly objectively dangerous, which caused the victim's death. Neither injury nor death was intended or foreseen, but the defendant intentionally carried out an unlawful and dangerous act which caused the victim's death.

The act must be intentional

KEY CASE: *DPP v Newbury and Jones* [1976] 2 WLR 918

Facts:

- Two young defendants pushed a concrete block over a railway bridge wall into the path of an oncoming train.
- The block crashed through the window and killed the guard.
- The House of Lords had to consider whether the defendants could be convicted of manslaughter where they did not foresee the harm their act may cause.

Lord Salmon held:

(a) an accused is guilty if it is proved that he intentionally did an act which was unlawful and dangerous and that act inadvertently caused death and
(b) that it is unnecessary to prove that the accused knew that the act was unlawful and dangerous.

Lord Salmon continued by explaining that not having to prove that the defendant knew the act was neither unlawful nor dangerous, accounted for why cases of manslaughter can vary in their seriousness from each other. They can, on the one hand be 'little more than pure inadvertence' and sometimes 'little less than murder'.

The act must be unlawful

The act which causes death must be not only intentional but also 'criminal' in the true sense. In *Fenton* (1830) 1 Law CC 179, throwing stones down a mine shaft was a civil wrong not a criminal act. However, the stones broke some scaffolding which killed a miner and the defendants were convicted of manslaughter. In contrast, in the later case of *Franklin* (1883) 15 Cox 163 the defendant threw a box over the pier at Brighton, killing a swimmer. Although the defendant was convicted, the case confirmed the general principle that a civil wrong should not lead to a criminal conviction.

Thus, there must be a criminal act which causes death. The prosecution cannot rely on the mere fact that death is caused, to conclude that the act which caused the death is criminal.

KEY CASE: *Lamb* [1967] 3 ALL ER 206

Facts:

- The appellant and his best friend were playing Russian roulette with a loaded revolver.
- The appellant believed there was no bullet in the chamber when he pulled the trigger, hence, it would be safe to fire.
- A revolver acts in such a way that the chamber of the revolver rotates, leaving the loaded chamber opposite the barrel.
- His friend was shot dead.
- The appellant appealed against his conviction for manslaughter.

Held:

Since both boys were 'larking' around, there was no assault. The appellant lacked intention and was not reckless. The *actus reus* also requires another to apprehend immediate and unlawful personal violence. As the friend believed it to be a game, there was no assault.

Since no criminal offence could be identified the appeal was allowed.

On-the-spot question

 Alex punches Ali in the face. Ali falls, hits his head on the pavement and dies. Could Alex be convicted of manslaughter?

Drug cases

There has been considerable academic debate as the whether a supplier of drugs can be held liable in manslaughter for the death of the victim to whom he supplies the drugs.

Historically, the position was reasonably straightforward. In the case of *Cato* [1976] 1 WLR 110, the defendant, who had injected his friend with heroin, had caused his death. The position became more complicated where the defendant prepared the drugs for the victim who then self injected. Here, the act of self injection effectively broke the chain of causation as in the case of *Dias* [2002] 2 Cr App R. The victim, who was an adult, was given the syringe, but it was his decision whether or not to inject the drugs.

However, the case of *Rodgers* [2003] 1 WLR 1374 can be distinguished from *Cato* as the defendant held a tourniquet around the victim's arm whilst he injected himself. Rodgers took an active part in the process. The Court of Appeal said no distinction could be made between a person who holds a tourniquet, allowing the other to self inject, and injecting the victim himself.

The current position of the law can be seen in the case below:

KEY CASE: *Kennedy* [2007] All ER 247

Facts:

- The defendant had supplied heroin to the victim.
- He had prepared the syringe and handed it to the victim to self inject.
- At first instance the defendant was convicted.
- The defendant appealed arguing that as self injection is not unlawful he could not be convicted of aiding and abetting self injection.

Held:

The House of Lords took the opportunity to simplify the law and held that 'it was never appropriate to find guilty of manslaughter a person . . . involved in the supply of a . . . controlled drug, which had . . . been voluntarily self-administered by the deceased'. Thus, a person cannot be guilty of unlawful act manslaughter where he prepares and hands the victim a filled syringe of heroin to self inject. It may be immoral, but it is not unlawful.

Cato (1976)	A person who injects another with drugs and causes their death will be liable for manslaughter
Dias (2002)	A person who hands a syringe of drugs to another in order for the victim to self inject will not be liable in manslaughter
Rodgers (2003)	A person who acts in the process of self injection by holding a tourniquet is liable for manslaughter
Kennedy (2007)	The law as it is today: if a person prepares drugs for another by supplying and preparing the syringe, they will not be liable for manslaughter if the victim self injects

The act must be dangerous

Unlawful act manslaughter also requires the act to be dangerous. It is a term which can be widely defined.

KEY CASE: *Church* [1965] 2 All ER

Facts:

- The appellant had sex with a woman in the back of his van.
- After sex, he assaulted her and she lost consciousness.
- When he could not revive her, he took her body out of the van and dumped it in a river in which she drowned.
- He appealed against his conviction for manslaughter arguing that he believed she was already dead when he threw her in the river. His appeal failed.

Held:

The Court of Appeal defined 'dangerous' widely and held as follows.

Per Lord Edmund-Davies, 'The unlawful act must be such that all reasonable and sober people would inevitably recognise it must subject the other person to, at least, the risk of some harm resulting therefrom, albeit not serious harm.'

Principle:

Whether an unlawful act is dangerous is objectively assessed and must involve the risk of harm being caused, although the harm does not necessarily have to be serious.

The case of *DPP v Newbury and Jones* [1976] AC 500 applied the objective test in *Church* and convicted the defendants even though the defendant may not have been able to appreciate the risk of physical injury due to their age. Given the way in which *Church* had defined whether a criminal act is dangerous, it was necessary to redefine the test in the cases we consider below.

KEY CASE: *Dawson* [1985] Cr App R 150

Facts:

- Dawson and a colleague carried out an armed robbery at a petrol station, wearing masks and carrying baseball bats.
- The employee, aged 50 who had a serious heart defect, suffered a heart attack and died.
- Dawson was convicted of manslaughter but his conviction was quashed on appeal.

Held:

The victim's heart defect would not have been known to a reasonable onlooker and therefore it was not obvious that the robbery posed a risk of some physical injury.

Thus, where the victim's frail condition is not obvious on an objective test, the defendant will not be liable in manslaughter. This principles runs somewhat contrary to the principles we have seen in causation (Chapter 2) where we learnt, for the purposes of murder we take a victim as we find them (*Blaue*), meaning a defendant's prior knowledge of any pre-existing condition is irrelevant.

KEY CASE: *Watson* [1989] 2 All ER 865

Facts:

- Watson and another entered the victim's house.
- He confronted the victim who was elderly, frail and suffered from a heart condition.
- They abused him verbally.
- 90 minutes later he died of a heart attack.

Held:

The Court of Appeal held that a reasonable person would have been aware of the physical condition of the victim once he entered the house. If one abuses an elderly, frail man with a heart condition, there is clearly a risk of some physical harm.

The conviction was quashed on the basis that causation could not be satisfied beyond reasonable doubt.

On-the-spot question

 Marcus breaks into Sanjay's house. He does not know Sanjay is upstairs, neither does he know that Sanjay is an elderly, frail man. Sanjay hears the break in, has a heart attack and dies. Is Marcus liable for Sanjay's manslaughter?

The act must cause death

The prosecution must be able to prove the defendant caused the victim's death; hence the normal rules of causation apply. We saw in the case of *Watson* above that the defendant's appeal was quashed as it was not possible to prove the defendant caused the victim's death. This principle is also relevant in the case of *Kennedy* where causation was not satisfied.

The act which causes death does not need to be directed at the victim

Although the defendant's act must be a direct cause of the victim's death in order to satisfy causation, the act need not be directed at the victim. In *Goodfellow* [1986] 83 Cr App R 23 the defendant maintained the victim's death was not the intended result of his arson. The Court of Appeal held all that had to be proved was that the defendant had intentionally carried out an unlawful and dangerous act which caused the victim's death. Whether or not they were the intended victim was entirely irrelevant.

GROSS NEGLIGENCE MANSLAUGHTER

Duty of care

The offence of gross negligence manslaughter is a common law offence which finds its roots in the civil law of tort. Here, the common law duty of care owed by one person to another is set down in the seminal case of *Donoghue v Stevenson* [1932] AC 562. The later case of *Caparo v Dickman* [1990] 2 AC 605 asked three questions before a duty of care could be established. The three questions it was necessary to address were as follows:

- Was there reasonable foreseeability between the parties that the claimant would be harmed?
- Was there proximity of relationship between the claimant and the defendant?
- Was it fair, just and reasonable to impose a duty on the defendant?

Where the duty of care in tort is breached, judged by objective standards, the defendant is liable and will be obliged to compensate the victim. In contrast, with gross negligence manslaughter, if death occurs as a result of that same breach of duty of care and the breach can be said to be 'grossly' negligent; the defendant can be criminally liable. The criminal standard is set higher than the civil standard due to the potential loss of reputation, livelihood and even liberty if the defendant is convicted. In reality, the criminal law does not expect the same application of the elements in *Caparo* above, although the case below illustrates the application of 'reasonably forseeable'.

KEY CASE: *Wacker* [2002] EWCA Crim 1944

Facts:

- The defendant, a lorry driver, was returning from Europe to the UK.
- In the sealed container there were 60 illegal immigrants.
- Whilst on the ferry, a small vent was sealed to eliminate any noise.
- Fifty-eight of the immigrants suffocated to death.

Held:

The court of first instance applied the rules of negligence and held that W owed the victims a duty of care. W appealed unsuccessfully against his conviction. The Court had determined that it was reasonably foreseeable that the victims would be affected by W's act.

The criminal requirements of gross negligence manslaughter

In order for the prosecution to successfully prove the offence of gross negligence manslaughter the following elements must be proved:

- The defendant must have owed the victim a duty of care.
- The duty of care must have been breached.
- The breach must have caused the death.
- The breach of duty of care was grossly negligent.

In order to secure a conviction, Lord Hewart held in *Bateman* [1925] 19 Cr App R 8 that the negligence must be so bad that compensation between the parties is inadequate and the defendant must be punished by the state. This principle was applied in *Andrews* [1937] AC 576 but thereafter remained largely unrecognised until the leading modern case of *Adomako* below.

KEY CASE: *Adomako* [1995] 1 AC 171

Facts:

- Adomako was an anaesthetist responsible for the patient during an operation.
- An essential tube supplying oxygen to the patient became disconnected.
- Adomako failed to notice or remedy the disconnection.
- The victim died.

Held:

Adomako was liable for gross negligence manslaughter as he owed a duty of care to the patient. The duty was breached when he failed to notice the tube had become disconnected. The failure had been the factual and legal cause of the victim's death.

When does a duty of care arise?

There is little difficulty in establishing that a duty of care arises between doctor and patient. However, unless a statutory duty of care arises, it is for the judge to determine whether a duty of care is imposed upon the defendant as shown in the cases below.

In *Singh* [1999] Crim LR 582, the victim had died from carbon monoxide poisoning from a faulty heater. The heater had been installed by the landlord and the fitter who owed the victim a duty of care to ensure the heater was fitted with the appropriate level of care and skill. There was a grossly negligent breach of the duty of care by the landlord's son in the landlord's absence to ensure the tenants were safe. The court held there must be an objective risk of death at the time of the breach of duty of care.

In the more recent case of *Willoughby* (2005) 1 Cr App R 29 the owner of a disused pub enlisted the help of another to set fire to it. The petrol which was used as an accelerant caused an explosion which killed the victim. W owed a duty of care, not because he was the owner of the pub but because he had asked the victim to assist him, which gave rise to the duty of care.

Omissions to act

Case law often illustrates gross negligence manslaughter in terms of an 'act', but gross negligence manslaughter can also be committed by an omission or a failure to act. In *Evans* [2009] EWCA Crim 650 the defendant was convicted when she failed to call an ambulance for the person to whom she supplied heroin, was taken severely ill. The court upheld her conviction maintaining that she was 'under a duty to take reasonable steps for the safety of the deceased once she appreciated that the heroin . . . was having a potentially fatal impact on her health'. More recently, and reminiscent of the case of *Stone v Dobinson* (see page 22), the defendant was convicted in *Barrass* [2011] EWCA Crim 2629 for failing to adequately care for his middle-aged sister with learning difficulties with whom he shared a house. His failure to provide for her needs and to summon help led to her death and his conviction for gross negligence manslaughter.

Breach of duty of care

Once the judge has decided as a matter of law whether there is a duty of care, it is for the jury to determine whether that duty has been breached. Since this is objectively tested, it is for the jury to decide whether the standard of care fell below that of a reasonable person endowed with that special skill and expertise.

Grossly negligent

What amounts to grossly negligent? Lord Mackay in *Adomako* said as follows:

> whether having regard to the risk of death involved, the conduct of the defendant was so bad in all the circumstances as to amount in their judgment to a criminal act or omission.

There is no clear definition of what amounts to a 'grossly negligent' act. Given the term is decided by the jury; inconsistent decisions could result. Clearly there is a circular theme; the defendant's negligence will be criminal if the act or omission is 'gross' but the jury are to decide for themselves whether the defendant's act or omission is sufficiently 'gross' to be criminal.

However, it is also necessary for the jury to consider the risk of death connected to the defendant's act or omission. In *Misra and Srivastava* [2005] 1 Cr App R 21 the defendant's patient had contracted a post-operative infection for which he was not treated and subsequently died. The defendant's conviction was upheld on the basis that there was an obvious risk of death; 'the circumstances must be such that a reasonably prudent person would have foreseen a serious and obvious risk not merely of injury, even serious injury, but of death'.

On-the-spot question

? A 15-year-old boy dies when a wall he was instructed to demolish collapsed. He had received no instruction and no supervision from H, who had employed him. Should the employer be liable for gross negligence manslaughter? The case of *Holtom* [2010] EWCA Crim 934 may help you decide.

You may also wish to consider why it has been observed that there is an overlap between the two forms of involuntary manslaughter.

Corporate manslaughter

As a result of the Corporate Manslaughter and Corporate Homicide Act 2007, companies and organisations can now be held liable for acts of gross negligence. The Act was introduced after a number of unsuccessful actions against companies in major disaster actions such as the King's Cross Fire Disaster (1987) and the Potters Bar Rail Disaster (2002).

Domestic Violence, Crime and Victims Act 2004

Section 5 sets out the offence of allowing the death of a child or vulnerable adult. It provides that an offence will be committed where, if two or more people share a house, a child or vulnerable adult with whom they have frequent contact, dies as a result of an unlawful act. Furthermore, the offence is extended to the person, who although not causing the death, ought to have been aware of the significant risk of serious physical being but took no steps to protect the victim.

SUMMARY

Murder

In this section, we have examined the common law definition of murder, as defined by Coke. We have also looked at the sentencing for murder on conviction, which is mandatory life. Finally, we have learnt that each of the four *actus reus* elements of the definition must be proved to obtain a conviction, although this is rarely a problem.

Unlawful act

In this section, we have seen that unlawful act manslaughter occurs where an unlawful homicide is carried without malice aforethought. The intentional act which the defendant carries out must be:

- Unlawful (in the criminal sense).
- Dangerous (objectively tested).
- And cause death (causation must be satisfied).

Gross negligence manslaughter

- A duty of care must exist between the parties, whether a duty of care exists is determined by the judge.
- The duty must be breached, causation must be satisfied and death must occur.
- The defendant's conduct must amount to gross negligence.

The negligence must be so 'gross' that compensation between the parties is inadequate and is deserving of criminal punishment, taking into account the risk of death involved.

FURTHER READING

Ashworth, A, 'Principles, Pragmatism and the Law Commission's Recommendations on Homicide Law Reform' [2007] Crim LR 333 – article considering reform of homicide.

Legislating the Criminal Code: Involuntary Manslaughter, Law Commission. No 237 – try reading the Law Commission report.

Herring, J and Palser, E, 'The Duty of Care in Gross Negligence Manslaughter' [2007] Crim LR 24 – article considering the law relating to gross negligence manslaughter.

www.telegraph.co.uk/health/healthnews/8195113/Disgraced-doctor-found-guilty-of-gross-negligence-manslaughter-allowed-to-practice-in-Germany.html.

COMPANION WEBSITE

An online glossary compiled by the authors is available on the companion website: www.routledge.com/cw/beginningthelaw

Chapter 5
Voluntary manslaughter

LEARNING OBJECTIVES

By the end of this chapter you should be able to:

- Understand and appreciate the common law of provocation
- Demonstrate an understanding of s 3 of the Homicide Act 1957
- Understand and demonstrate a clear understanding of the Coroners and Justice Act 2009 and the new partial defence of loss of control
- Be able to understand the common law of diminished responsibility
- Understand the provisions under the Homicide Act 1957 and the Coroners and Justice Act 2009

THE NEW LAW OF LOSS OF SELF CONTROL AND THE OLD LAW OF PROVOCATION

Introduction

Voluntary manslaughter occurs when the defendant is charged with murder but pleads one of the four special defences, loss of self control, diminished responsibility, infanticide or suicide pact. The chapter will focus primarily on loss of self control and diminished responsibility.

If the defendant successfully relies on loss of self control (formerly provocation) and diminished responsibility as a defence, it has the effect of reducing the verdict from murder to manslaughter. These defences are only available to the offence of murder although may be used as a mitigating factor in sentencing in other offences.

If convicted of voluntary manslaughter the defendant:

- admits he committed the *actus reus* of the victim (caused the death)
- admits the *mens rea* (the intention to kill or to cause GBH)
- but successfully pleads one of the special defences.

Why do we have this special defence? The law attempts to distinguish between killings which are conducted when a person is truly provoked or suffers from an 'abnormality of mental functioning' and those murders committed in revenge or 'cold blood' for which there is no defence. The Coroners and Justice Act 2009 prevents the defence being relied upon 'if the D acted in a considered desire for revenge' section 54(4).

Loss of self control (formerly provocation)

Background

Provocation was a historical offence, created by common law and dating back to the seventeenth century. Due to inconsistencies, s 3 of the Homicide Act 1957 put provocation on a statutory footing. Although now referred to as 'loss of self control' and contained in the Coroners and Justice Act 2009, the development of case law concerning provocation remains crucial in our understanding of the modern-day law of loss of self control.

Devlin J in *Duffy* [1949] 1 All ER 932 explained provocation as amounting to:

> some act or series of acts done by the dead man to the D which would cause in any reasonable person, and actually caused in the D, a sudden and temporary loss of self control rendering him so subject to passion as to make him for the moment not master of his mind.

The case of *Richens* (1994) 98 Cr App R 43 confirmed the defendant does not need to have lost total control, just enough that he 'is unable to restrain himself from what he is doing'.

Section 3 of the Homicide Act 1957 explained that where a person is charged with murder it is for the jury to determine whether the person was provoked (by actions or words or both) so as to lose his self control. It is then for the jury to decide whether a reasonable man would have acted in the way he did. If he did, he will not be convicted of manslaughter.

The Coroners and Justice Act 2009 came into force in October 2010 and introduced a new defence of 'loss of self control'. The current requirements of loss of self control are contained in s 54 of the Coroners and Justice Act 2009 which states that:

> 1) Where a person (D) kills or is party to a killing of another (V), D is not to be convicted of murder if –
>
>   a)   D's act and omissions in doing or being a party to the killing resulted from D's loss of self control,
>   b)   the loss of self-control had a qualifying trigger, and
>   c)   a person of D's age and sex, with a normal degree of tolerance and self restraint and in the circumstances of D, might have reacted in the same or in a similar way to D.

By virtue of the Coroners and Justice Act 2009, s 54(5), the onus is on the prosecution to disprove the defence of provocation once it is before the jury. It is, however, the judge's role to initially determine whether there is sufficient evidence of loss of self control to be put before the jury (s 54(6)).

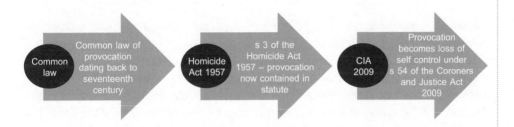

Provoking words or conduct

Historically, there was no requirement that provoking words or conduct had to be illegal in nature (*Doughty* (1986) 83 Cr App R 319, where the persistent crying of a baby amounted to provoking words or conduct).

'Sudden' loss of self control

Under the common law and the Homicide Act 1957, there had to be evidence of a *sudden and temporary loss of self control at the time of the killing;* a subjective test to be determined by the jury.

The requirement of a *sudden* loss of self control raised the issue of where there was a time delay between the last provocative words or conduct and the killing; a 'cooling off period'. Clearly, the longer the time period between the provocation and the killing, the more it would appear to a jury the killing was an act of revenge or a premeditated killing contrary to the concept of the defence being a *'concession to human frailty'* – *Smith (Morgan James)* [2000] 4 All ER 289. Indeed, the case of *Ibrams and Gregory* (1981) 74 Cr App R 154 held that a delay of five days between the last provocation and the killing of the provoker was held to be inconsistent with the defence of provocation.

Under the common law and the Homicide Act 1957, the requirement of a *sudden* loss of self control meant that victims of 'battered spouse syndrome' were often unable to successfully plead provocation. In *Thornton (No 1)* [1992] 1 All ER 306, the defendant sharpened a knife in the kitchen before killing her husband. This evidence of a 'cooling off' period was held to negate the defence of provocation. These defendants (victims in their own right) often planned to kill their spouse after a long and sustained history of mental and physical abuse.

The case of *Ahluwalia* (1993) 96 Cr App R 133 illustrates the other historic difficulty as in 'battered spouse' cases there was not necessarily a *sudden* loss of self control but a cumulative effect of a number of episodes. The court allowed the appeal although accepted that the longer the delay between the provocative words or conduct and the act that leads to the victim's death, the more likely it was that the defence of provocation would fail.

Although the courts had recognised the importance of cumulative provocation and the relevance of the background to what triggers the *actus reus* (see *Thornton (No 2)* [1966] 2 All ER 1023, the new statutory provisions in s 54(1)(c) of the Coroners and Justice Act 2009 explains that the defendant must be judged as someone '*in the circumstances of the defendant'*. The jury can now take account of *all* the circumstances of the defendant's case together with the history of anything they may have suffered at the hands of the victim. The new Coroners and Justice Act, s 54(2) states it does not matter whether the loss of self control is sudden or not.

'Qualifying trigger'

Section 54(1)(b) states the loss of self control must have a qualifying trigger. Section 55(2) of the Coroners and Justice Act 2009 explains a loss of self control has a qualifying trigger if subsection (3), (4) or (5) applies. This section helps to assist in understanding what amounts to a provocative act. It may now be that the persistent crying baby (*Doughty*) would no longer amount to a provocative act (which many would feel is morally correct). Section 3 suggests reference to the 'battered spouse', although the use of the word 'fear' may discriminate against men who are likely to be less fearful of their spouse than women.

The table below shows the provisions of ss 55(3)–(5) of the Coroners and Justice Act 2009 (emphasis added).

s 55(3)	Applies if the D's loss of self control was attributable to D's fear of *serious violence* from V against D or another identified person
s 55(4)	Applies if D's loss of self control was attributable to a *thing or things done or said (or both)* which . . .
s 55(4)(a)	constitutes circumstances of an *extremely grave nature*
s 55(4)(b)	causes the D to have a justifiable sense of being *seriously wronged*
s 55(5)	Applies if the D's loss of self control was attributable to a combination of the above

Factors excluded from the 'qualifying trigger'
Section 55(6)(c) states '*the fact that a thing done or said constituted sexual infidelity is to be disregarded'* when considering the defendant's loss of self control.

> ### Example
>
> Mark returns home to find his wife in bed with his best friend, Roger. Blinded by rage and tormented by betrayal, Mark kills Roger. Prior to the Coroners and Justice Act 2009, this would have amounted to provocation to be taken into account but, since the introduction of s 55(6)(c), sexual infidelity is not to be regarded. In *Clinton (Jon Jacques)* [2012] EWCA Crim 2 the appellant killed his wife and was, at first instance, convicted of her murder on the basis that sexual infidelity was not relevant to the defendant's loss of self control. On appeal, however, the court explained that the Coroners and Justice Act does not permit infidelity to be used as a 'qualifying trigger' capable in itself of causing someone to lose their self control *but* it can be taken into account as part of the circumstances which at the time of the killing have to be examined.

The reasonable man; who is he and where has he gone?

Section 3 of the Homicide Act 1957 referred to the 'reasonable man' as the standard against whom the defendant's behaviour would be judged. The reasonable man was described as a person of the defendant's age and sex, with a normal degree of tolerance and self restraint and in the circumstances of the defendant. In other words, the jury would ask themselves whether a reasonable defendant, so provoked would have responded the way the defendant did.

The common law extended the identity of the 'reasonable man' until the case of *Smith* which culminated in a reasonable man being subjective rather than objective as intended by the Homicide Act 1957. The development of the common law is shown in the table below.

Bedder (1954)	No allowance was made for characteristics which may affect a person's self control; the reasonable man was not impotent
Camplin (1978)	Bedder reversed. The age and sex of the defendant (in this case a 15-year-old boy) should be taken into account when considering how a reasonable man would react to the provocation. Age and sex could also be taken into account when assessing the *level of self control* to be expected of the reasonable man
Morhall (1995)	House of Lords held that any characteristic which affects the *gravity of the provocation* are relevant when determining who the reasonable man is. Here, the reasonable man was a glue sniffer which should be taken into account

---

KEY CASE: *Smith (Morgan James)* **[2000] 3 All ER 289**

Facts:

- The defendant suffered from severe depression.
- The defendant killed the victim following an argument over a set of tools.
- He argued his depression affected his ability to exercise self control.

Held:

The House of Lords upheld the decision of the Court of Appeal maintaining it was for the jury to decide whether the defendant's depression was relevant to the objective test. They rejected the distinction between loss of self control characteristics and gravity characteristics and with the exception of male possessiveness, jealously, obsession, violent rages or childish tantrums, all other characteristics could be taken into account.

Thus, the reasonable man ceased to exist. The case was followed by a seminal Privy Council case in 2005 which redrew the boundaries of provocation and returned the law to the parameters set by *Camplin* in 1978.

KEY CASE: *Attorney General for Jersey v Holley* **[2005] UKPC 23**

Facts:

- The defendant, an alcoholic, killed his girlfriend after she admitted having sexual relations with another man.
- The Court of Appeal allowed his appeal against his conviction for her murder accepting his argument that his chronic alcoholism (not drunkenness) should be taken into account when considering whether his loss of self control was excusable.

Held:

On appeal, the Privy Council held alcoholism was not a characteristic to be taken into account. To do so would be a distortion of s 3 of the Homicide Act 1957 which, since *Smith*, had almost entirely departed from the objective test.

As a result of *Holley*, only the *age and sex* was to be taken into account when determining how a reasonable man would have acted, but *any* characteristic could be taken into account when considering the gravity of the provocation.

Although *Holley*, a Privy Council case, is not binding on decisions in England and Wales, subsequent cases such as *Mohammed (Faqir)* [2005] EWCA Crim 1880 and *Karimi and James* [2006] EWCA Crim 14, both followed the decision in *Holley* rather than *Smith*.

The Coroners and Justice Act 2009 does not make any reference to the reasonable man. Instead, s 54(1)(c) refers to the 'ordinary' man, who is *'D's age and sex, with a normal degree of tolerance and self restraint and in the circumstance of D, might have reacted in a similar way to D'*. Hence, the Coroners and Justice Act 2009 reverts the law to the pre-*Smith* position of loss of self control, ensuring an objective test but still permitting, under s 54(1)(c), characteristics of the defendant to be taken into account as far as the gravity of the provocation is concerned.

On-the-spot question

 Orwina is a drug addict and is continually taunted for being a red-head by Albert. She stabs Albert in a fit of rage. Albert dies. Would this amount to provocation for the purposes of the Homicide Act 1957?

Under *Smith*, the fact that she is a drug addict would be a characteristic that would be taken into account when determining whether the reasonable man would have lost his control the way Orwina did. The taunts would probably satisfy the gravity of provocation. Under *Holley* the reasonable man is only endowed with the characteristics of the age and sex of the defendant. The Coroners and Justice Act 2009 reflects the decision in *Holley*. Orwina may also be able to argue under s 55(4)(a) that her loss of self control was attributable to things said which were of an extremely grave nature and caused her to have a justifiable sense of being seriously wronged. It is however, a question for the jury to determine.

DIMINISHED RESPONSIBILITY

Introduction

Much like loss of control, diminished responsibility, if successfully pleaded, will reduce a conviction of murder to one of manslaughter. A successful plea does not entitle the defendant to be acquitted altogether.

Diminished responsibility was contained in the Homicide Act 1957 (s 2) as a response to criticism of the narrow definition of the common law of insanity under the M'Naughten Rules of 1843.

The purpose of the defence of diminished responsibility is to permit the operation of mental disorder conditions falling short of pure insanity but extending beyond simple extreme emotions. It is quite correct that a person who, for reason of a mental disorder, commits a murder should be less morally culpable than one who does not suffer so.

Even though diminished responsibility was introduced, the defence of insanity remains and the two offences exist as distinct separate offences, with insanity being much narrower in its scope than diminished responsibility. Insanity is a defence which applies to defendants who do not appreciate and understand the act they are committing, or do, but do not know that it is wrong. Diminished responsibility allows a defendant to know and appreciate that it is wrong to kill the victim but still avail himself of a defence.

Unlike loss of self control, where the evidential burden rests on the prosecution to disprove the defence, with diminished responsibility, the defendant must be able to prove the elements of the defence on a balance of probabilities (*Dunbar* [1958] 1 QB 1 and (s 2(2) of the Homicide Act 1957). Given the nature of the defence, there must be medical evidence to support the defendant's '*abnormality of the mind*' – *Dix* (1981) 74 Cr App R 306.

Section 52 of the Coroners and Justice Act 2009 repeals s 2 of the Homicide Act 1957. However, it is still necessary to have a thorough knowledge of its provisions together with the common law as they will have considerable influence on the interpretation of the Coroners and Justice Act 2009.

Diminished responsibility under the Homicide Act 1957

Key Definition

Section 2(1) of the Homicide Act stated:

Where a person kills or is a party to the killing of another, he shall not be convicted of murder if he was suffering from such abnormality of mind (whether arising from a condition of arrested or retarded development of mind or any inherent causes or induced by disease or injury) as substantially impaired his mental responsibility for his acts or omissions in doing so or being party to the killing.

The elements of s 2(1) can be broken down for ease of reference and understanding to:

- there must be an *abnormality of the mind* arising from arrested development, or inherent causes or disease or injury; and
- that abnormality must result in *substantial impairment of mental responsibility* for the defendant's actions, and
- the abnormality must have been a *substantial cause* of the defendant's act.

The Coroners and Justice Act 2009

Section 52 of the Coroners and Justice Act 2009 (CJA) amends s 2 of the Homicide Act 1957 by changing the definitions of what amounts to a person with diminished responsibility. The changes in the wording are simply to assist with clarity and, in reality, the defence changes little with the new legislation.

The table below compares and contrasts the old law under s 2 of the Homicide Act 1957 with the new provisions under CJA 2009, s 52.

s 2 Homicide Act 1957	s 52 CJA 2009
Abnormality of mind	Abnormality of mental functioning
Arrested or retarded development of mind, or any inherent causes or induced by disease or injury	Refers to a recognised medical condition. Must substantially impair the defendant's ability to understand the nature of his conduct, form a rational judgement, or exercise self-control
Substantial impairment of D's mental responsibility for the killing	Must cause, or is a significant contributory factor in causing, the defendant to carry out the conduct

'Abnormality of the mind' under the Homicide Act 1957

The difficulty with the term 'abnormality of the mind' is that it was not only wide but also vague in its definition. This is demonstrated in the case below.

KEY CASE: *Byrne* [1960] 2 QB 396

Facts:

- The defendant strangled a young woman and then mutilated her body.
- He was convicted of murder but, on appeal, his conviction was quashed and manslaughter on the grounds of diminished responsibility substituted.
- Evidence was submitted that the defendant had uncontrollable violent and /or sexual impulses and desires that it was difficult to control.

Held:

Lord Parker CJ explained as follows: 'Abnormality of the mind . . . means a state of mind so different from that of ordinary human beings that the reasonable man would term it abnormal. It appears to us to be wide enough to cover the mind's activities in all its aspects, not only the perception of physical acts and matters and the ability to form a rational judgement whether an act is right or wrong, but also the ability to exercise will-power to control physical acts in accordance with that rational judgement.'

The table below shows 'conditions' that have been held to fulfil the requirement of 'abnormality of the mind'.

Price (1971)	Allowed in 'mercy killing' where the defendant, who suffered from depression so as to amount to abnormality of the mind, killed his severely handicapped son
Vinagre (1979)	Unfounded jealously that his wife was having an affair amounted, somewhat tenuously, to a disease of the mind
Gittens (1984)	Chronic depression amounted to an abnormality of the mind, regardless of whether he had been taking drugs or consuming alcohol
Seers (1984)	The defendant, who had chronic reactive depression, killed his wife. Even though it was not an 'inherent cause' the defence was allowed
Campbell (1987)	Appellant successfully relied upon epilepsy as an abnormality of the mind sufficient to lessen his responsibility for his fatal act
Hobson (1998)	Battered women's syndrome
Reynolds (1988)	Pre-menstrual syndrome was allowed where a woman killed her mother

Ahluwalia (1992)	Following a 10 year history of domestic violence, a woman killed her husband by throwing petrol in his bedroom and setting him alight. We considered this case in provocation but, on appeal, she submitted evidence of a depressive disorder and her murder conviction was quashed following a successful plea of diminished responsibility
Martin (Anthony Edwards) (2001)	Successfully relied on diminished responsibility on appeal against a murder conviction. He shot two burglars on his deserted Norfolk farm, one in the back. He provided evidence of a paranoid personality disorder sufficient to be considered as an abnormality of the mind

The complication of voluntary intoxication

In Chapter 6 you will learn that intoxication can, on occasions, be a defence to specific intent crime. It is never a defence to basic intent crimes where recklessness forms the *mens rea*. If the defendant kills whilst drunk but relies on diminished responsibility; does the intoxication render the defence unavailable? There is also an issue between the distinction of intoxication and chronic alcoholism. If the alcoholism has led to a disease of the brain, it will, in fact, amount to 'abnormality of the mind'.

In *Tandy* (1988) 87 Cr App R 45, having consumed a bottle of vodka, the appellant, an alcoholic, killed her daughter after she found out she had been sexually abused. She was convicted of murder but appealed arguing her alcoholism amounted to an 'abnormality of the mind', therefore she could avail herself of the defence. In order to prove alcoholism should come within s 2, she needed to prove first, that alcoholism had injured the brain so as to impair her judgement and second, that her alcoholism was so severe that it was tantamount to being involuntary.

The common law becomes more complex where there are two or more causes of abnormality of the mind, one of which is intoxication. In these circumstances, it is necessary for the jury to ignore the intoxication altogether and ask whether, if the defendant was not intoxicated, he would have:

- killed as he in fact did;
- still be under diminished responsibility when he did so?

Thus, the defendant had to be so affected by the intoxication that it amounted to an abnormality of the mind within s 2 so as to reduce the mental responsibility of the act.

KEY CASE: *Dietschmann* [2003] UKHL 10

Facts:

- D was a heavy drinker and due to depression also had a prescription for anti-depressants and sleeping tablets.
- He killed his friend after an argument and pleaded diminished responsibility.
- Medical evidence showed he was suffering from mental illness brought on by the death of his aunt.
- He appealed against his conviction to the House of Lords.

Held:

The House of Lords ruled the defence of diminished responsibility could still be open to the defendant, even if the defendant would not have killed if he had been sober.

In one of the first cases to deal with the new statutory provisions, the case below confirms the approach taken by the courts under the Homicide Act 1957.

KEY CASE: *Dowds (Stephen Andrew)* [2012] EWCA 281

Facts:

- The defendant was a heavy drinker.
- He had been drinking when he killed his girlfriend in a frenzied knife attack following an argument.
- He reported her death to the police two days later.
- The trial judge ruled that his intoxication precluded the defence of diminished responsibility.
- On appeal, he maintained that intoxication was a recognised medical condition which satisfied CJA, s 52 and therefore diminished responsibility should have been left to the jury.

Held:

The court held that the Coroners and Justice Act 2009 had not reversed the principle that voluntary acute intoxication could not be relied upon in diminished responsibility.

Whilst it was necessary to establish a 'recognised medical condition', it was not always enough upon which to raise a defence.

INFANTICIDE

Section 1(1) of the Infanticide Act 1938 as amended by s 57 of the Coroners and Justice Act 2009 allows a woman who:

- causes her child's death
- by act or omissions
- when the child is under 12 months of age

to rely on the defence of infanticide, if she can provide evidence that her:

balance of her mind was disturbed by reason of her not having fully recovered from the effect of giving birth to the child or by reason of the effect of lactation consequent upon the birth of the child.

A conviction of infanticide is 'as if she had been guilty of the offence of manslaughter' and can be sentenced to the maximum of life imprisonment.

Whilst infanticide can be regarded as an offence, it can also be seen as a defence and a woman permits a woman who kills her child within the first 12 months of her child's life to argue that her balance of her mind was disturbed from childbirth.

SUICIDE

Suicide is no longer an offence, having been abolished by s 1 of the Suicide Act 1961. The offence of aiding, abetting, counsel and procuring a suicide remains an offence by virtue of s 2(1) of the Suicide Act 1961. The new offence under s 2A of the Suicide Act 1961, created by s 59 of the Coroners and Justice Act 2009, simply consolidates s 1(1) of the Criminal Attempts Act 1981 and s 2(1) of the Suicide Act 1961. There are no significant changes to the wording. This area of the criminal law, although it receives a cursory mention here, is probably one of the most controversial but topical issues of the decade.

What amounts to assisting a suicide?

The case of *Attorney General v Able* [1984] 1 QB 795 held that a publication by the voluntary euthanasia society outlining ways in which one could end their life, could not be considered aiding and abetting, unless a clear connection could be established between the supply of the book and the person considering suicide with the intent of assisting or encouraging him.

Suicide pact

Section 4(3) of the Homicide Act 1957 defines a suicide pact as a 'common agreement between two or more persons having for its object the death of all of them'. Section 4(1) states that, in these circumstances, a manslaughter charge rather than a murder charge is appropriate.

SUMMARY

Provocation

- Provocation was historically a common law defence which was modified by s 3 of the Homicide Act 1957.
- The Coroners and Justice Act 2009 abolishes common law provocation and repeals s 3 of the Homicide Act 1957.
- It is for the judge to decide whether there is evidence of loss of control to be put before the jury.
- The jury must decide whether the defendant lost control and whether the loss of self control had a qualifying trigger.
- The jury must also decide whether the ordinary man (as the same age and sex as the defendant) would have acted the way the defendant did.

Diminished responsibility

- Diminished responsibility is a defence distinct from insanity.
- Section 2 of the Homicide Act 1957 sets out the requirements for the defence which, if successful, will result in a conviction for manslaughter.
- It was necessary to establish an abnormality of the defendant's mind which substantially impairs the defendant's mental responsibility for the killing.
- Section 52 of the Coroners and Justice Act 2009 amends the definitions.

- Section 52 now refers to an abnormality of the mental functioning (a recognised medical condition) which substantially impairs the defendant's ability to either understand his actions or to exercise self control.
- The abnormality of the mental functioning must cause, or is a significant contributory factor in causing, the defendant to carry out the conduct.

ISSUES TO THINK ABOUT FURTHER

Consider whether the new law on loss of self control will ensure that the law represents a true 'concession to human frailty', as provocation was originally designed to do. Ensure you can support your opinion with reference to case law.

FURTHER READING

Ashworth, A, 'Homicide: Coroners and Justice Act 2009 section 54 – loss of control – qualifying trigger' [2012] Crim LR 539–44 – a case commentary in light of the case of *R v Clinton (Jon-Jacques)* [2012] EWCA Crim 2.

Ashworth, A, 'R v Dowds: diminished responsibility – murder – amendment of the Homicide Act 1957 s.2 by the Coroners and Justice Act 2009' [2012] Crim LR 612–14 – a case commentary in light of the case of *R v Dowds (Stephen Andrew)* [2012] EWCA Crim 281.

www.legislation.gov.uk/ukpga/2009/25/contents – the Coroners and Justice Act 2009.

COMPANION WEBSITE

An online glossary compiled by the authors is available on the companion website: www.routledge.com/cw/beginningthelaw

Chapter 6
Defences – duress, necessity, self defence, mistake and intoxication

LEARNING OBJECTIVES

By the end of the chapter you should be able to:

- Understand the concept of criminal defences in English law
- Be aware of the difference between excusatory and jusificatory defences and the different rational behind each
- Appreciate the basic workings of the general defences of duress, necessity, self defence, mistake and intoxication
- Be able to discuss the problems which arise around these defences and the common law which has arisen around them

INTRODUCTION

It can be seen from the diagram below that the issue of a defence is crucial in criminal law. If a defendant successfully pleads a defence, he is not guilty of the crime, in spite of the fact that he performed the requisite *actus reus* with the requisite *mens rea*.

JUSTIFICATORY OR EXCUSATORY?

A criminal defence can be either **justificatory** or **excusatory**. If a defence is justified, it means that although the *mens rea* and *actus reus* elements of the offence are present, the person was justified in acting as they did in those circumstances and their actions will not consitute a criminal offence. This leads to an acquittal for the accused person, and, as no crime as been committed, to an acquittal for anyone who might have also been charged, for instance with aiding or abetting the offence. Self defence is a justificatory defence.

> ## Example
>
> Joe accuses Satnam of flirting with his girlfriend in a coffee shop. Joe punches Satnam, who punches Joe back. James, who is sitting nearby, leaps up and holds Joe away from Satnam. Joe is furious and accuses both Satnam and James of battery.
>
> Satnam and James will be able to plead self defence to the charge – see below – Satnam because he was defending himself, and James because he was defending another, or because he was acting to prevent a crime. Both will be acquitted of any criminal charge. Joe – of course – may be convicted of battery or s 47 of the Offences Against the Person Act 1861.

An excusatory defence is one which will still acquit the defendant, but for a different reason. The defendant acknowledges he has committed the requisite *actus reus* with the required *mens rea*, but maintains that anybody would have acted as he did in those particular circumstances, and therefore he should be excused any punishment for his offence. These defences admit that a crime has been committed, and therefore anyone who has acted with the accused but does not have a defence can still be found guilty. These defences are ususally subject to the 'reasonable man' test, to ensure that other people would have acted in the same way in the same circumstances. Duress is an excusatory defence.

> ## Example
>
> Peter threatens to kill Jody unless she drives the getaway car for a bank robbery he means to commit. Frightened, Jody agrees, but they are both caught and charged with the offence. Jody may use the defence of duress – see below – and be excused the punishment she would have faced. Peter is guilty of the offence as charged.

SELF DEFENCE

Self defence is a general defence, which means it can be used as a defence for any offence against property, or the person, from murder to common assault. It can be pleaded if a person has used reasonable force to protect himself, or another person from attack, or property from damage or distruction. Self defence is a common law defence, but there has been an attempt to clarify it under s 76 of the Criminal Justice and Immigration Act 2008.

Defence of the person

Common law cases have established several rules that are true for someone who seeks to use self defence. The case of *Bird* [1985] 1 WLR 816 states that there is no 'duty to retreat' when under attack by another. Historically, the defendant in a case would have to show they tried not to fight by trying to get away from the assault before being forced to react with violence. The case of *Beckford* [1988] AC 130 establishes that the use of a **'pre-emptive strike'** is still conducive to the defence of self defence. This means that if A fears attack by another, it is not fatal to his defence if he lands the first blow.

Self defence proceeds on the basis of what was the **honest belief** of the defendant.

KEY CASE: *Gladstone Williams* [1984] Crim LR 163

Facts:

* Williams saw two men fighting on the street.
* He tried to help the 'losing' man, C, by applying force to the assailant, F.
* Williams was charged with assault occasioning actual bodily harm.
* It turned out that F was a policeman trying to lawfully arrest C.

Held:

At first instance, the jury were directed that they could only acquit Williams if he had a 'reasonable belief' that F was acting unlawfully. This was overturned on appeal. The Court of Appeal held that Williams had a defence if he 'honestly believed' he was acting in defence of C – whether this belief was reasonable or not.

The modern test for self defence is found in the case of *Oatridge* [1992] Crim LR 205. When the defence is raised, three questions should be asked:

1. Was the defendant under actual or threatened attack by the victim (or did he honestly believe himself to be – see *Gladstone Williams* above)?
2. If the answer to the first question is yes, did the defendant act to defend himself against this attack?
3. If yes, was his response commensurate with the degree of danger created by the attack?

The first test is subjective. It proceeds purely on the honest belief of the defendant. If the defendant honestly believed himself to be under attack by the victim, then the jury must look at the situation from that point of view, even if the defendant was mistaken. The second test is also subjective, but the third is objective. It is for the jury to decide if the defendant used 'reasonable force' in the situation in which he believed himself to be.

Example

Sabeela is out shooting when she sees Penny who is about to kick her in the shin. Sabeela shoots Penny dead. In this situation, it is not reasonable for Sabeela to respond with such disproportionate force. Even though the first two parts of the *Oatridge* test are satisfied, Sabeela would fail on the third and be found guilty of – probably – murder (remember Coke's definition?).

Drunken self defence

If a person makes a mistake as to the need to use self defence because they are intoxicated by drugs or alcohol, then they cannot use the defence. This is supported by the cases of *O'Grady* [1987] 3 WLR 321 and *O'Conner* [1991] Crim LR 135

Defence of property

If a defendant used force against a person in defence of property, he may be able to rely on s 3(1) of the Criminal Law Act 1967. This section reads:

> A person may use such force as is reasonable in the circumstances in the prevention of crime, or in effecting or assisting in the lawful arrest of offenders or suspected offenders or of persons unlawfully at large.

Example

David is in his front garden playing with his pet dog, Reb. A man leans over the garden wall, picks Reb up and begins to walk away with him. David gives chase and rugby tackles the man, causing him to fall and giving him a black eye and split lip.

It is likely that David will be able to use the defence in s 3(1), because he is preventing the theft of his dog, who is his property. Remember that the force used must still be reasonable – if David had used a knife to stab the man he may have been convicted of an offence against the person, but most people would think it reasonable to try to stop a person stealing a family pet by tackling him as David did.

An all or nothing defence?

One of the problems with self defence is that it is an 'all or nothing' defence. It either succeeds and there is a complete **acquittal**, or it fails absolutely. It is not difficult to imagine a situation where a person was under genuine attack by another, but, in the heat and fear of the moment, responded with more force than was objectively necessary. If self defence fails this defendant, they are liable to be convicted and sentenced for the full offence, which in the case of murder could be life imprisonment. It has been suggested that in cases like this there should be a conviction for a lesser offence such as manslaughter, to reflect the decreased culpability of the defendant, although presently this does not happen.

DURESS

Duress is an excusatory defence. It can be pleaded when the defendant admits that they committed the crime with the relevant *mens rea* and *actus reus*, but only did so because they had been threatened with death or serious injury if they did not do so. The threats relied on must be of 'immediate harm' but need not be threats against the defendant. In the case of *Conway* [1988] 3 All ER 1025 the threat made was against a passenger in the defendant's car. The defendant could then use the defence against a charge of driving dangerously as he tried to get his passenger away from the potential assailant.

The test for duress, and against what crimes it can be pleaded, has shifted over recent years.

Lord Lane formulated a two-stage test to be applied by the jury when they were considering whether or not the defence could be relied upon by the defendant. It comes from the case of *Graham* [1982] 1 All ER 801.

KEY CASE: *Graham* [1982] 1 All ER 801

Facts:

- The defendant was a homosexual man who lived with his wife and another homosexual man, K.
- The defendant was taking drugs because of anxiety attacks and these made him susceptible to bullying.
- K was jealous of the defendant's wife and put an electrical flex around her neck, telling the defendant to pull it tight.
- The defendant did and the wife died.
- At his trial for murder, the defendant pleaded the defence of duress.

Held:

Lord Lane gave this two-stage test to the jury:

1. Was the accused, or may he have been, impelled to act as he did because, as a result of what he reasonably believed the person issuing the threat had said or done, he had good cause to fear that if he did not so act that person would kill him or cause him serious personal injury?
2. If so, have the prosecution made the jury sure that a sober person of reasonable firmness, sharing the characteristics of the accused, would not have responded to whatever he reasonably believed the person making the threat said or did by taking part in the killing. The fact that an accused's will to resist has been eroded by the voluntary consumption of drink or drugs, or both is not relevant to this test.

Note here that the defence in the first test rests on 'reasonable' and not 'honest' belief. As duress is a complete defence, and the defendant will be excused a possible life sentence in jail if sucessful, it is important that society feels it can understand why he acted in the way he did. The second test makes it clear that once the defence is raised it is for the prosecution to disprove the duress, and not for the defence to prove it. The second test also uses the 'reasonable man' as a standard against which the defendant is to be measured. The jury must feel that anyone in that situation would have acted the same way as the defendant, and therefore he does not deserve criminal punishment.

Characteristics of the 'reasonable man'

Which of the defendent's characteristics should be attributed to the reasonable man is controversial – remember the discussion for 'loss of control'? In the second test, Lord Lane states that intoxication is to be disregarded. Other than that, the case of *Bowen* (1996) 2 Cr App R 157 makes it clear that the reasonable man is very reasonable indeed! Lord Justice Stuart-Smith listed the characteristics that could be taken into account as – 'Age, possibly sex, pregnancy, serious physical disability, recognised mental illness or psychiatric condition.' He went on to say 'the mere fact that the accused is more pliable, vulnerable, timid or susceptible to threats than a normal person does not amount to a characteristic to attribute to the reasonable person, and psychiatric evidence is not admissible on this matter'. *Bowen* concerned a man with an IQ of just 68 – the average in the UK is between 100 and 110. This was held not to be a relevant characteristic which made him less able to withstand threats or pressure.

The House of Lords (now the Supreme Court) decision in the case of *Hasan* is the latest clarification to the law in this area.

KEY CASE: *In the case of Hasan* [2005] UKHL 22

Facts:

- The defendant, armed with a knife, forced entry into a house with the intention of stealing from a safe known to be inside.
- He was charged with aggravated burglary (on account of the weapon).
- He pleaded the defence of duress.
- He claimed that a man called Sullivan, a drug dealer with a reputation for violence, had threatened to harm him and his family if he did not carry out the burglary.
- The defendant worked as a driver for a woman who was involved in prostitution, and Sullivan was the employer's boyfriend.

Held:

At first instance Hasan was convicted. He could not use duress as a defence because he had voluntarily associated with criminals.

The Court of Appeal overturned his conviction on the grounds that Hasan did not forsee that he would be threatened if he did not commit burglary (as opposed to another crime).

> The House of Lords (now the Supreme Court) reinstated his conviction, holding that it was enough if Hasan was voluntarily associated with criminals and could foresee that he 'may be the subject of compulsion by them or their associates'.

The House of Lords (Lord Bingham) also summarised the elements of the defence:

1.   duress is no defence to murder, attempted murder or treason;
2.   there must be a threat of death or serious injury;
3.   the threat must be directed against D or his immediate family or someone close to him, or someone for whom D would reasonably regard himself as responsible;
4.   D's perception of the threat and his conduct in response must be objectively assessed;
5.   the conduct which the duress is sought to excuse must be directly caused by the threats D relies on;
6.   there must be no evasive action D could reasonably take; and
7.   D cannot rely on duress to which he has voluntarily laid himself open.

Duress cannot be a defence to murder as established in the case of *Howe* [1987] 1 All ER 771. If the defence could be used, this would imply that the law should hold the defendant's life to be more important than the victim's, and this cannot be the case. If threatened with death unless you commit a murder, the law says you must die! The same is true of attempted murder, as illustrated by the case of *Gotts* [1992] 2 WLR 284. The seventh point from Hasan concerns defendants who have voluntarily joined or become associated with criminals. Hasan makes it clear – building upon previous case law such as *Heath* [2000] Crim LR 109 and *Harmer* [2002] Crim LR 401 – that those who do associate with criminals should foresee they could be subject to pressure from such people to commit crimes, and therefore the defence of duress is unavailable to them.

NECESSITY

Traditionally, there has been no defence of necessity in English criminal law. This dates back to the (in)famous case of *Dudley & Stephens* (1884–5) LR 14 QBD 273.

KEY CASE: *Dudley & Stephens* (1884–5) LR 14 QBD 273

Facts:

- The two defendants were members of a ship's crew (Dudley was the captain).
- The ship – The Mignonette – was wrecked and sunk off the Cape of Good Hope about 1,100km from the nearest land.
- Dudley, Stephens, another man called Brooks and a cabin boy, Parker, managed to get into a lifeboat in which they drifted with very little food and water for 19 days.
- Parker fell into a coma and the other three men, having wives and children to support, decided to kill him and eat his body to enable them to survive. It was common ground that without the nourishment obtained, it is unlikely Dudley, Stephens and Brooks would have survived.
- The surviving men were picked up by a passing boat five days later.
- The survivors believed they were protected by a custom of the sea accepted at the time that it was better for one person to die than for all to perish. They were quite open with the truth of what happened to Parker, and apologised to his family.

Held:

To their suprise, and popular outrage, Dudley and Stephens were charged with and convicted of murder on the high seas. They had pleaded the defence of necessity, but this was rejected by the judge, Baron Huddleston.

After a complicated legal process and trial, they were sentenced to death, but this was reduced to six months imprisonment.

This case has been used as precedent ever since to establish that necessity is not a relevant defence in English law. If necessity was a defence it could be argued, then the door would be opened to all sorts of people to plead that their need was greater than another's and on balance, they should be excused punishment.

Example

It is a very cold winter and Sharon is homeless and hungry. She sees an open window on the ground floor of Phillip's house and climbs in. She makes herself a cup of hot tea and a sandwich. When Phillip comes home he calls the police and Sharon is arrested.

If necessity was a general defence, it would be hard to argue that Sharon should be punished for her actions. She has caused no damage and her 'need' for the food is greater than Phillip's.

This was part of the common law of England and Wales until the case of *Re A* [2001] 2 WLR 480.

KEY CASE: *Re A* [2001] 2 WLR 480

Facts:

- A woman from Malta came to the UK for the birth of her conjoined twins.
- One of the little girls', J, was a fully functioning child in relatively good health.
- The other child, M, had no functioning heart or lungs, and an underdeveloped brain.
- Because the girls' circulatory systems were joined, J's heart and lungs were pumping oxygenated blood around M's body as well.
- Doctors warned this stress would result in J's heart failure and death for both babies within six months.
- Doctors wanted to separate the girls to give J the chance of a normal life. It was accepted that if the operation went ahead, M would die as she had little organ function.
- The girls' parents opposed the operation and the case went to court.

Held:

The Court decided that if the doctors did operate to separate the twins, knowing that M would die, this would be murder. However, the defence of necessity would be open to the doctors.

The judge was careful to restrict use of the defence to the facts of the case.

This means that the defence can only be used in a similar case, where the separation of conjoined twins will inevitably result in the death of one of the children. Although this is very restrictive, it allows necessity as a defence back into English law.

INTOXICATION

Intoxication it not a true defence under English law. It is a denial of the *mens rea* of the offence. A defendant may claim that he was so intoxicated – by drugs or alcohol – that he was simply unable to form the necessary *mens rea* required. Although this may sound like a reasonable claim as it is important that *actus reus* and *mens rea* are present, a general application of intoxication as a defence would lead to some obvious problems! A criminal would simply be able to intentionally take alcohol or drugs before committing a crime, and then if he got caught would be able to claim a defence. Most people would not feel this was appropriate and the law would be brought into disrepute.

English law has found a way around this tension between lack of *mens rea* and public confidence by way of the rule in *Majewski* [1977] AC 443.

WARNING! This rule applies only to voluntary intoxication!

KEY CASE: *Majewski* [1977] AC 443

Facts:

- Majewski became intoxicated by taking a mixture of alcohol and drugs.
- While intoxicated he punched a man, cut another with broken glass and hit a police officer.
- When charged with assault offences, he argued that he was so drunk he did not know what he was doing and therefore did not have the *mens rea* for the offences.

Held:

His case was eventually decided by the House of Lords (now the Supreme Court), who held that a defendant who becomes voluntarily intoxicated must be held responsible for his conduct while in that condition.

The rule developed in this case states that intoxication **can** be pleaded as a denial of *mens rea*, but only to offences of **Specific Intent**. These are offences which require intention as the *mens rea*, such as murder or s 18 of the Offences Against the Person Act 1861. Intoxication **cannot** be pleaded to offences of **Basic Intent**. These are offences which require either intention or recklessness as a *mens rea*, such as s 20 or s 47 of the Offences Against the Person Act 1861. In these cases, said Lord Elwyn-Jones in *Majewski*:

His course of conduct in reducing himself by drink and drugs to that condition in my view supplies the evidence of *mens rea*, of guilty mind certainly sufficient for crimes of basic intent. It is a reckless course of conduct and recklessness is enough to constitute the necessary *mens rea* in assault cases.

This means that if a person commits a crime which can be committed recklessly while they are intoxicated, the recklessness which they exhibited in getting drunk is transferred to form the recklessness required for the *mens rea* of the crime. The *mens rea* then does not have to be proven separately by the prosecution, it is enough that the *actus reus* can be proven beyond reasonable doubt.

Example

Grace goes out with friends and drinks heavily. She wakes up in a police cell with no idea how she got there. Later, the police interview her and show a CCTV tape of Grace fighting angrily with a woman in the street. The woman is seriously hurt. Grace is very upset and tells the police she remembers nothing and would not have intended to harm the woman, who is a stranger to Grace. The police would not charge Grace with a s 18 Offences Against the Person offence as it would be difficult to prove her intention to cause GBH. She would be charged with a s 20 offence, one that can be committed recklessly. (Remember the definition of 'Maliciously'?) Her recklessness in getting drunk would form the *mens rea* of the offence – even though she remembers nothing of the fight.

This may not seem fair. Earlier in this book we discussed how an act had to be voluntary to be a part of an *actus reus*, and the fact that there must be a coincidence between *actus reus* and *mens rea*. Neither of these two things seem to be present here. If Grace really cannot remember fighting, was it voluntary, or was she acting as an automaton? If she was reckless in getting drunk earlier in the evening, how does that match up with the criminal act of fighting much later? The courts seem to accept in the case of intoxication that some elements of the rules of criminal law will be bent by the *Majewski* rule, but consider that the rule is necessary on the grounds of policy and protection of the public.

Involuntary intoxication

This occurs when a person does not set out to consume intoxicants, but takes them unwittingly. This might be because someone has 'spiked' their drink, or they have had an unusual reaction to a drug prescribed to them by a doctor. In this situation, intoxication can be used as a denial of *mens rea* for **all** offences. The defendant will only be acquitted however, if he genuinely did not have the intent or recklessness required. In the case of *Kingston* [1995] 2 AC 355 it was established that an intoxicated intent to indecently assault a boy was nevertheless an intent, and the defendant should be convicted in spite of the fact that his drink had been laced with a drug, and the situation involving the boy had been set up to provide evidence by which the defendant could be blackmailed.

MISTAKE

It is easy to see how a defendant charged with a crime may plead that he had simply made a mistake and did not intend to break the law. Whether his mistake is relevant as regards his innocence will depend on what sort of mistake it is.

Mistake as to what the criminal law is will not be relevant. If a defendant thinks there is no speed limit on British motorways and so drives at 90 miles an hour, he will still be guilty, even if he genuinely does not know the speed limit is 70 miles an hour.

Mistake of fact

Where the defendant has made a factual mistake, this may negate his *mens rea* for that particular offence.

Example

Maggie takes a coat from the rack after she has finished eating at a restaurant. She thinks it is hers, but actually it is a similar one, belonging to Kate.

In this case, Maggie's factual mistake about the ownership of the coat means that she does not have the dishonesty *mens rea* element to make her guilty of theft. All other elements are present, Maggie has appropriated property belonging to another and intends to permanently deprive the other of it. Her belief that the coat is her own, although mistaken, means that she is not dishonest.

Mistake as to a defence

A situation may arise where a defendant uses a defence in error. He may think he is under attack, or being threatened, when that is not – in fact – the case. In these situations, whether the defendant can rely upon the mistake will differ depending on whether the defence he used is a justificatory one, or an excusatory one.

- If the defence is justificatory – like self defence – the mistake must be honestly held by the defendant, but need not be reasonable. It is a subjective test only.
- If the defence is excusatory – like duress – the mistake must be both honest and reasonable. It has subjective and objective components.

SUMMARY

- The lack of a defence forms the essential 'third element' in criminal liability alongside the *actus reus* and the *mens rea*.
- The general defences discussed in this chapter can be pleaded against any criminal charge, except when specifically excluded by case law, such as the exclusion of duress as a defence to a charge of murder or attempted murder.
- Defences can be justificatory or excusatory. Although it is sometimes not clear which catagory a defence falls into, it can be important in terms of the liability of accessories, or the test for mistaken use of the defence.
- Self defence is a common law, justificatory defence – the three-part test is found under *Oatridge* (1992).
- The closely related defence found in s 3(1) of the Criminal Law Act 1967 allows a person to use reasonable force in the prevention of a crime or to assist lawful arrest.
- Duress, an excusatory defence, can only be pleaded when a person fears immediate death or serious injury if they do not commit a crime.
- The two-stage test is taken from *Graham*, the characteristics of the reasonable defendant are restricted to the list in *Bowen*.
- In the case of *Hasan*, the House of Lords laid out the modern restraints on the use of duress as a defence.
- Necessity is a very restricted defence in English law. It is a complete defence, but is restricted to the facts of the case of *Re A (Conjoined twins)* (2001).
- Intoxication is not a defence but a denial of *mens rea*. Voluntary intoxication is governed by the *Majewski* test.
- Involuntary intoxication is not governed by the *Majewski* test. In this case the intoxication will operate to negate *mens rea* where the *mens rea* was not – in fact – formed. Intoxicated intent is still intent.

- If a defendant makes a mistake of fact, it may negate the *mens rea* for the crime, leading to no liability.
- If the mistake is as to the need to use a defence, whether this is a relevant mistake will depend on the defence pleaded. A justificatory defence will require only honest (subjective) belief in the mistake made, an excusatory defence will require both honest and reasonable belief to be present.

KEY CASES

Case	Legal principle
Oatridge (1992)	Sets out the three-stage test for self defence
Glanville Williams (1984)	A mistake as to the need to use self defence only needs to be honestly held
O'Grady (1982)	A drunken mistake is not a relevant mistake for self defence
Graham (1982)	Sets out the two-stage test for duress
Bowen (1996)	Lists permitted characteristics of the 'reasonable person' for duress
Hasan (2005)	The modern overview of duress (H of L)
Dudley & Stephens (1884) (note date)	There is no defence of necessity under English law
Re: A (Conjoined twins) (2001)	Necessity restricted to the facts of this case
Majewski (1977)	Intoxication is irrelevant for offences of basic intent
Kingston (1995)	(Involuntary) intoxicated intent is still intent

ISSUES TO THINK ABOUT FURTHER

Self defence is an 'all or nothing' defence. If a person, in the heat of the moment and under attack, uses beyond what is later considered to be 'reasonable force' and the 'victim' dies, the defendant gets a mandatory life sentence and is labelled a murderer. It has been suggested there should be a 'partial defence' in self defence as well, so that the jury would be entitled to find that the defendant was justified in using self defence, but had not used reasonable force in the circumstances. The jury would then be able to convict the defendant of manslaughter instead of murder.

It is easy to see why duress is not a defence to murder, as the law must hold all life equally valuable. Duress is even denied as a defence if a person is told that if they do not comply with the order to commit a crime their family and children will be killed. It seems especially harsh to then condemn a person who (thinks he) is acting to preserve the lives of innocent people, even if an innocent person will be a victim. If duress is a 'concession to human frailty' then the threat of the death of spouse and family must be one of the few things that most humans would kill for.

It seems unfair that involuntary intoxication isn't allowed as a genuine defence. If a person does not know they are taking an intoxicating substance they have no chance to prevent or limit their consumption. In the case of *Kingston*, the defendant was aware of his weaknesses and did not drink or allow himself to be around young men on his own. In spite of this he was found guilty because of an intention he formed when he was given alcohol surreptitiously – an intention he would not have formed without the alcohol.

The *Majewski* rule is controversial because it assumes that the recklessness exhibited in becoming intoxicated can be 'moved' to form the *mens rea* of any basic intent criminal offence committed while under that intoxication. As very few people go out with the intention of committing a crime, even if they intend to get drunk, this is a difficult stretch for the law to make. This sort of public policy may lead to unjustifiable and disproportionate charge and sentencing as most crimes have a 'basic' form that will be easily charged if someone is intoxicated.

FURTHER READING

Simester, A, 'Intoxication is never a defence' [2009] Crim LR 3 – a short editorial about the Law Commission's proposals for clarifying the confusion over 'specific' and 'basic' intent and the relationship to intoxication.

Yeo, S, 'Killing in defence of property' (2000) 150 NLJ 730 – a brief, but interesting, article comparing the Australian approach to defence of property with the English case of Tony Martin.

Padfield, N, 'Duress, Necessity and the Law Commission' [1992] Crim LR 778–89 – an older, but still relevant article about the proposed codification of the law of necessity and duress.

Ormerod, D, 'Duress: Foreseeability of risk of being subjected to compulsion by threats of violence' [2006] Crim LR 142–6 – facts and commentary on the key case of Hasan with discussion on the D's voluntary exposure to threats by joining a criminal gang.

COMPANION WEBSITE

An online glossary compiled by the authors is available on the companion website: www.routledge.com/cw/beginningthelaw

Chapter 7
Non fatal offences against the person

LEARNING OBJECTIVES

By the end of this chapter you should be able to:

- Appreciate that there are five main non fatal offences against the person
- Know that two are common law offences defined by case law and three are statutory offences under the Offences Against the Person Act 1861 (OAPA 1861)
- Know they are usually used to charge someone who has injured another person
- Understand some of the problems with the law that have arisen due to the age of the OAPA 1861 and the language it contains
- Understand that the law now encompasses 'new' forms of injury such as psychological injury

INTRODUCTION

The non fatal offences are used to charge someone who has injured another person, but the victim has not died. If a defendant injures another person – even accidentally – who then dies of their injuries, a charge of manslaughter or murder may lie, depending on the state of mind of the defendant. The non fatal offences cover a very wide range of actions and consequences, from a raised fist and a threat of violence, to just short of attempted murder (see Chapters 3 and 10). At first sight, some of these offences seem to criminalise very trivial behaviour and minor harm. They are offences however because the law takes very seriously any interference with a person's physical integrity. Everyone has a right not to feel threatened or to be touched against their will. The non fatal offences uphold this right, but note that it is not protected by a new statute, but very old common law and a statute from the middle of the nineteenth century!

Each of the non fatal offences will be looked at individually and its *mens rea* and *actus reus* examined. Remember all of the elements of a crime must be present for the crime to be committed, and there must be no defences available to the defendant for a successful prosecution. In the case of non fatal offences, a person may well plead self defence as a defence to the criminal charge. For more on self defence, see Chapter 6.

Offence	Derived from
Assault	Common law – charged under s 39 of the Criminal Justice Act 1988
Battery	Common law – charged under s 39 of the Criminal Justice Act 1988
Assault occasioning actual bodily harm	s 47 of the Offences Against the Person Act 1861
Grievous bodily harm or malicious wounding	s 20 of the Offences Against the Person Act 1861
Grievous bodily harm or wounding with intent to do grievous bodily harm or wound	s 18 of the Offences Against the Person Act 1861

COMMON LAW OFFENCES

Assault

Assault is sometimes charged alongside battery as 'assault and battery' or 'common assault' on a charge sheet. In spite of this, assault is a separate crime at common law. Confusingly, the word assault is also sometimes used as a shorthand form of 'assault and battery'! Here we will use the word assault to mean 'pure assault' where there is no physical contact with the victim.

The classification of assault as a summary offence (triable at the magistrates' court only), and the penalty for the crime is laid down in s 39 of the Criminal Justice Act 1988. This reads:

> s 39 – Common assault and battery to be summary offences.
>
> Common assault and battery shall be summary offences and a person guilty of either of them shall be liable to a fine not exceeding level 5 on the standard scale, to imprisonment for a term not exceeding six months, or to both.

Assault is not defined in a statute. It is such an ancient crime that its beginnings are lost in the history of the legal system. However, the law takes the definition of the elements of assault from case law.

Key Definitions

actus reus – any act that causes another to apprehend immediate, unlawful, personal violence (case of *Fagan* [1968] 3 All ER 442)

mens rea – intention or (*Cunningham*) recklessness that another should apprehend immediate, unlawful, personal violence (case of *Venna* [1975] 3 All ER 788).

Actus reus

Violence
It is important to note that there doesn't actually have to BE any violence, just the apprehension that it is about to occur. Shaking a raised fist at a person or threatening them by words alone can be enough to satisfy a charge. In the case of *Lamb* [1967] 2 QBD 981 a man laughed and joked as his friend pointed a gun at him. Neither of them knew the gun was loaded and when the friend 'pretended' to fire the gun, the man was killed. It was held there had been no assault (for the purposes of unlawful act manslaughter – see Chapter 5), because there had been no apprehension of violence.

Immediate
Immediate violence does not mean that the victim must apprehend that the violence could be carried out there and then. The courts have interpreted this word generously. There does however have to be a fairly short span of time in which the violence may happen.

Example

Dave, a passer-by, knocks into James at the railway station, causing James to spill his coffee. James runs after Dave, waving his fist and threatening to kill him. Dave jumps onto a train just as the doors are closing, leaving James on the platform, still shouting.

This situation would not be considered 'immediate'. Dave knows he is safe from any threat of violence from James. This assumes Dave and James are strangers. If James lived next door to Dave and there was another train very shortly, the situation may be different.

For instance, in the case of *Lewis* [1970] Crim LR 647, CA, there was held to be the threat of 'immediate' violence even though the victim was behind a locked door through which the defendant had no access.

Apprehension

There is no need for the victim to be afraid. The word apprehension simply means that a person can see something is about to happen. A masochist who is a willing victim of violence would apprehend violence even while welcoming it. A person who is asleep could not apprehend violence and therefore could not be a victim of 'pure assault'.

Mens rea

The *mens rea* of assault is either intention – direct or indirect (as defined in *Nedrick/Woollin*) – or recklessness. This is *Cunningham* recklessness which is subjective – refresh your memory by taking another look at Chapter 2.

On-the-spot question

Sahid is walking along the street when his friend, Will, comes along and hits him on the back of the head. Is this an assault?

(Remember the legal definition of the word.)

Battery

Battery is also a common law offence charged under s 39 of the Criminal Justice Act 1988 (see above). Battery usually suggests that someone has been beaten up or at least injured, but in fact the victim does not have to suffer any harm at all. The legal definition comes from the case of *Faulkner v Talbot* [1981] 1 WLR 1528.

Key Definition

Any intentional [or reckless] touching without the consent of that person and without lawful excuse. It need not necessarily be hostile or rude or aggressive, as some of the cases seem to indicate.

Actus reus

The *actus reus* of battery is the application of unwanted, unlawful force to the victim. It can be applied directly or indirectly.

In the case of *Haystead v DPP* (2000) 2 Cr App R 339 a man hit a woman who then dropped the child she was holding. The defendant was found guilty of battery of the child also. There was a direct battery of the woman and an indirect battery of the child.

Unwanted force inflicted on another may be lawful, such as in cases where a person is acting in self defence or where a police officer is acting in the line of duty.

Mens rea

The *mens rea* of battery is intention to apply unwanted, unlawful force to another, or being reckless as to whether that force is unwanted. The definitions of intention and reckless are the same as for assault (above).

> **Example**
>
> Dick sees a person who he thinks is his old friend Jane. He rushes up to her and hugs her. The woman is not Jane and is very distressed. Although here the touching is unwanted by the victim, Dick does not intend this, nor is he reckless as he is sure the woman is Jane. With no *mens rea*, there is no crime.

Assault occasioning actual bodily harm

This offence is found under s 47 of the Offences Against the Person Act 1861. It will be charged when there has been an assault OR a battery on another which results in some physical harm to the person. The Crown Prosecution Service (CPS) has advised prosecutors that the following may be suitable for a s 47 charge:

- the loss or breaking of a tooth or teeth;
- temporary loss of sensory function, including loss of consciousness;
- extensive or multiple bruising;
- a displaced broken nose;
- minor fractures of bones;
- minor (but not superficial) cuts requiring medical treatment;
- a recognised psychiatric disorder.

Causing any of these injuries (by assault or battery) would constitute the *actus reus* of assault occasioning actual bodily harm. The CPS goes on to say that grazes, minor bruising, swelling, superficial cuts or a black eye should normally be prosecuted as common assault – meaning 'assault and battery'.

The case of *Miller* [1954] 2 QB 282 gives the key definition for actual bodily harm:

Key Definition

Any hurt of injury calculated to interfere with the health and comfort of the victim.

In the case of *Smith* [2006] 1 WLR 386 it was held that even cutting a person's hair without their consent can amount to ABH. The judge said:

> Even if, medically and scientifically speaking, the hair above the surface of the scalp is no more than dead tissue, it remains part of the body and is attached to it. While it is so attached, in my judgment it falls within the meaning of 'bodily' in the phrase 'actual bodily harm'. It is concerned with the body of the individual victim.

The Offences Against the Person Act is now 150 years old and our understanding of the word 'injury' is now more sophisticated than it was then. The law recognises that 'bodily injury' can include psychological injury resulting in a diagnosed mental illness such as depression or an anxiety disorder. This was recognised in the joined cases of *Ireland and Burstow* [1997] 4 All ER 225.

KEY CASE: *Ireland and Burstow* [1997] 4 All ER 225

Facts:

- Ireland was charged with causing ABH to a woman whom he subjected to a prolonged period of 'stalking behaviour'.
- He made silent 'phone calls and waited outside the woman's house.
- Burstow was charged with grievous bodily harm (GBH – see below), for also stalking a female victim.
- Burstow stole items of underwear from the woman's washing line.
- He scattered condoms in her garden.
- He made silent and threatening 'phone calls and waited outside her house and outside her children's school.
- Both women suffered depression and anxiety as a result of the behaviour and were under the care of their doctors.

Held:

These cases were both cases on appeal to the House of Lords (now the Supreme Court) and were concerned with the definition of the word 'bodily'. This is why they were held together as a joined case. The appellants argued that the women victims had not suffered 'bodily harm' as required by the charges because they had not been physically molested by the appellants.

The Court upheld the charges against the men and dismissed the appeal. The Court held that the brain was as much part of the body as any other organ and was as susceptible to damage as any other. Psychological harm is now accepted as both ABH and GBH, provided there is a diagnosis from a doctor or psychiatrist. The Court in Ireland and Burstow was clear that 'mere emotions' were not within the remit of the OAPA.

Example

Rohit receives some unpleasent emails from his ex-girlfriend Melissa. He becomes very worried and is unwilling to open his email. Unless Rohit becomes mentally ill as a result of his worry, there is no offence here under the OAPA 1861. His concerns are 'mere emotion'.

Mens rea of s 47

The *mens rea* of assault occasioning actual bodily harm (ABH) is the same as the *mens rea* for assault or battery. This means that as long as a person intends or is reckless as to the assault or battery, there is no need for him to intend the ABH which is occasioned.

This is demonstrated clearly in the case of *Savage* [1992] 4 All ER 698 in which a woman saw her ex-boyfriend in a pub with his new girlfriend. There was an argument and the woman threw a drink over the girlfriend. As she did so the glass slipped from her hand and the girlfriend was cut on the cheek by broken glass. The woman was charged with ABH under s 47 but contended that while she had meant to throw the drink, she had not meant to throw the glass, nor had she seen the risk of the glass breaking and cutting the victim's cheek.

The court held that 'extra' *mens rea* was not necessary. The *mens rea* for s 47 and for the battery were the same.

> ### Example
>
> Bonnie pushes Bruce during an argument. Bruce falls backwards and sprains his ankle. As long as Bonnie intended the battery (the push) then she can be found guilty of a s 47 offence. She does not have to intend, or be reckless as to, the injury suffered by Bruce (the sprained ankle).

Some would argue that it is unfair to a defendant to make him criminally responsible for something he did not foresee would happen and did not intend. This argument is stronger when you realise that the maximum sentence of imprisonment for a battery (the push) is six months, but for s 47 (the sprained ankle) it can be up to five years. Yet in both cases the defendant's actions and intentions (*actus reus* and *mens rea*) are the same. A counter-argument might be that if a defendant is prepared to interfere with another's bodily integrity, then they must bear the blame for the consequence of that interference.

Inflicting grievous bodily harm or wounding

This offence is charged under s 20 of the Offences Against the Person Act 1861.

Section 20 reads:

> whosoever shall unlawfully and maliciously wound or inflict any grievous bodily harm on any other person, either with or without a weapon or instrument, shall be guilty of a misdemeanor.

Again we can see that the use of the word 'unlawfully' suggests there can be a lawful infliction of GBH, for instance under self defence. Section 20 is a triable either way offence with a maximum sentence of six months imprisonment and/or a fine not exceeding the statutory maximum if found guilty summarily (in front of a magistrate) or of five years imprisonment or an unlimited fine if found guilty on indictment (by a jury at the Crown Court)

Actus reus

Wounding
The *actus reus* of s 20 can be either wounding or infliction of GBH. A wound has a precise legal definition from the case of *C v Eisenhower* [1984] QB 331.

In this case a boy was hit in the eye with a pellet from a gun, causing a severely bloodshot eye. It was held that the injury was not a 'wound' as this required 'both the inner and outer layers of skin to be broken'. In *Eisenhower's* case, although a membrane had been ruptured internally, causing the bloodshot eye, there was no break in the outer layer of the skin (or eye) – so there was no wound.

Example

Phil punches Tim in the stomach. When Tim is taken to hospital a scan reveals a ruptured spleen which is bleeding heavily. Tim needs a blood transfusion and an operation to remove the spleen. Phil cannot be charged with wounding under s 20 as the blood loss was internal. Depending on his state of mind, he could still be charged with GBH – see below.

Grievous bodily harm

Grievous is another archaic word that is not now in common use, but reflects the age of the statute. Like ABH it has had to be redefined by case law for the modern age. In the case of *Smith* [1961] AC 290, HL the judges decided that grievous meant 'really serious'. In the later case of *Saunders* [1985] Crim LR 230 this definition was adjusted. It was decided that the word 'really' in the definition of grievous 'added nothing'. Therefore the meaning we are left with is that GBH means 'serious bodily harm'. It is for the jury to decide whether the harm suffered by the victim is serious, but – as for ABH – the CPS charging standards give some guidance for prosecutors. An injury is likely to be charged as s 20 if it includes:

- injury resulting in permanent disability, loss of sensory function or visible disfigurement;
- broken or displaced limbs or bones, including fractured skull, compound fractures, broken cheek bone, jaw, ribs, etc;
- injuries which cause substantial loss of blood, usually necessitating a transfusion or result in lengthy treatment or incapacity;
- serious psychiatric injury. As with assault occasioning actual bodily harm, appropriate expert evidence is essential to prove the injury.

On-the-spot question

Rose is devastated when her boyfriend Kenny dumps her. Rose send letters and emails to Kenny, pleading with him to get back with her, sometimes dozens a day. She also sends flowers, bottles of his favourite wine, and designer clothes which she thinks he will like. When she begins to wait outside his house to beg him to go out with her again, Kenny speaks to his doctor. He is very anxious and unable to sleep – he is also afraid to go outside in case Rose is waiting for him. The doctor gives Kenny anti-depressants and arranges an appointment with a psychiatrist. Is Rose guilty of an offence under the OATP 1861?

Tip: Think about all the elements of an offence before you decide!

Infliction

In s 20 of the Offences Against the Person Act 1861 (OAPA), the GBH must be 'inflicted'. This led defendants to argue that they had not inflicted harm if there was consent to the action that resulted in the harm. In the old case of *Clarence* (1888) 22 QBD 23 a wife complained of GBH where her husband had given her a sexually transmitted disease. It was held that the harm had not been inflicted, because the wife had agreed willingly to the sex that led to the disease being transmitted. This is clearly a decision of its time. It is easy to see that there is a huge question mark over the wife's true consent. She did agree to sex with her husband, but she did not agree to sex with her husband carrying a sexually transmitted disease! Had she been in possession of the full facts, she may not have agreed to the act.

The case of *Wilson* [1996] AC 242, HL made the Court consider whether 'infliction' was a term with only unpleasant connotations. Traditionally it might be said that punishment was inflicted, but the term would not be used for a neutral or happy event. Picking five correct numbers on the National Lottery would not be said to inflict a win on someone for instance. It would cause a win. The word 'cause' is used in s 18 of the OAPA in relation to intentional wounding, or GBH, so it was argued that because the draftsmen of the Act used two different words, different meanings must be intended. The Court held that the words 'inflict' and 'cause' in ss 18 and 20 meant the same thing and there was no need for 'inflict' to denote an unpleasant act and 'cause' a neutral one.

In the much more recent case of *Dica* (2003) 2 Cr App R 28 a man tried to plead the defence of consent to the charge of GBH for infecting his female partners with the HIV virus which can lead to AIDS. Like *Clarence*, he pleaded that his partners had been willing to have sex with him. In a clear indication of the modernisation of the law in this area, the Court held that the women could not have consented as they were not fully aware of what they were consenting to. They did consent to sex with the defendant, but not to unprotected sex with a man who was HIV positive. If they had known they may have made a different decision.

Mens rea

The *mens rea* of s 20 is 'maliciously'. This is a word that has a precise legal definition which may not match the everyday use to which the word is generally put. In the case of *Mowatt*

[1968] 1 QB 421 it was held that malicious means the intention or recklessness as to the causing of 'some harm, not necessarily the level of harm that was in fact caused'. In this case, what is important is the legal principle behind the case. Here the legal principle is the definition of malicious.

> ### Example
>
> Sahira hits Jenny with a wooden post, hoping Jenny will be too bruised and uncomfortable to go on a date that night. Jenny's arm is badly broken in three places. Sahira is guilty of GBH under s 20 if she foresaw 'some harm' would be caused as a result of hitting Jenny with the post. It does not matter that Sahira did not intend the GBH and anticipated only bruising.

Causing grievous bodily harm or wounding

This offence is charged under s18 of the Offences Against the Person Act 1861.

Section 18 reads:

> Whosoever shall unlawfully and maliciously by any means whatsoever wound or cause any grievous bodily harm to any person, . . . with intent, . . . to do some . . . grievous bodily harm to any person, or with intent to resist or prevent the lawful apprehension or detainer of any person, shall be guilty of felony, and being convicted thereof shall be liable . . . to be kept in penal servitude for life.

Again, the use of the word 'unlawfully' in this section confirms that there will be instances where such force can be used lawfully. Self defence is a defence for all the offences under the Offences Against the Person Act 1861. A s 18 offence is triable only on indictment, that is before the Crown Court, and the maximum sentence is life imprisonment. This is not a mandatory sentence – as it is for murder – but at the discretion of the judge.

Actus reus

The *actus reus* of the s 18 offence is the same as for the s 20 offence. 'Wound' and 'grievous bodily harm' have the same definitions. Note that the injury has to be 'caused' and not 'inflicted' as mentioned previously. The court has held in *Wilson* that these two words mean the same thing.

Don't forget that the offences against the person have to satisfy the three rules of causation as part of the *actus reus* (see Chapter 2).

Mens rea

The *mens rea* of s 18 is intention only. This can mean direct or oblique intention as defined under the *Nedrick/Woollin* test. Refresh your memory by taking another look at Chapter 2 if you need to.

Two offences, two intentions
If you look carefully, there are two separate offences in s 18. One is:

> Whosoever shall unlawfully and maliciously by any means whatsoever wound or cause any grievous bodily harm to any person, . . . with intent, . . . to do some . . . grievous bodily harm to any person.

This closely mirrors the s 20 offence, apart from the intention only *mens rea*. In addition:

> With intent to resist or prevent the lawful apprehension or detainer of any person, [commits GBH or wounds] shall be guilty of felony, and being convicted thereof shall be liable . . . to be kept in penal servitude for life.

Notice where the requirement of intent lies in these offences. For the first offence, the intention has to be to wound, or to cause the GBH. This is similar to the s 20 element which we looked at previously. For the second offence, the intention is NOT to cause the injury to the person, but to resist arrest or prevent the lawful apprehension or detention of another. If that intention is present, there is no need for intention as to the GBH or wound. Recklessness is sufficient.

CONSENT

People are taken to have consented to what might technically be a battery when it occurs as part of everyday life. Everyone is jostled on a busy high street or may be squashed up against someone else on a packed tube train.

In certain situations, the law allows a person to consent to bodily injury that would otherwise be illegal. If this were not the case, a dentist would not be allowed to extract a rotten tooth, as this would be at least ABH. The law allows for consent in two separate categories.

1. Where a person can consent to bodily injury that **will** occur. This will cover situations such as surgery, or ear piercing or tattooing.
2. Where a person can consent to bodily injury that **may** occur, even though he hopes it will not. This will cover situations such as properly conducted sports and games, or rough horseplay.

Both of these categories can be added to 'in the public interest'.

Think back to the cases of *Wilson* and *Brown*. The injury caused in *Wilson*, with the hot knife was held to be a 'bodily adornment' and likened to a tattoo. The injuries in *Brown*, although they carried no permanent damage, could not be consented to by the 'victims' as 'the satisfaction of a sadomasochistic libido is not in the public interest'.

SUMMARY

The five offences we have studied in this section are not difficult in themselves, but they each carry their own distinct *actus reus* and *mens rea* requirements, which you will have to remember. Assault, battery, s 47 and s 20 all have the same *mens rea* requirement of intention or *Cunningham* recklessness, but s18 is satisfied by intention only – either to commit GBH, or to resist arrest/prevent lawful detention. Look at the table below and remember the *actus reus* of the offences. There are some peculiar things to watch out for.

- The *mens rea* for s 47 is the **same** as for the assault or battery on which the offence is based. As long as the assault or battery *mens rea* is present it is **not necessary** for the D to intend or be reckless as to any injury suffered by V.
- There is **no need** for an assault or battery for a conviction for ss 18 or 20 – although often there will be one. This is shown in cases such as *Dica*.
- These offences now include psychiatric harm, and even hair cutting without consent – contrast this with consensual harm such as in *Wilson*.
- The maximum sentences for s 47 and s 20 are the same. This is so even though the level of harm for s 20 should be so much higher.

KEY CASES

Case	Legal principle
Fagan (1968)	Legal definition of the *actus reus* of assault – 'an act which causes another to apprehend immediate, unlawful, personal violence'
Faulkner v Talbot (1981)	Legal definition of *actus reus* of battery – 'any unwanted touching'
Miller (1954)	Definition of actual bodily harm – 'any hurt or injury calculated to interfere with the health and comfort of V'

Ireland and Burstow (1997)	Acceptance of psychiatric injury as 'bodily harm'
Savage, Parmenter (1992)	No additional *mens rea* requirement for a s 47 offence from an assault or battery
Eisenhower v C (1984)	Definition of a wound – 'a break in both the inner and outer layers of the skin'
Smith (1961)	Definition of grievous in GBH – 'really serious harm'
Mowatt (1968)	Legal definition of malicious – 'intention or recklessness as to the causing of some harm, not necessarily the level of harm in fact suffered'

ISSUES TO THINK ABOUT FURTHER

You should now appreciate that the age of the Offences Against the Person Act 1861 has caused problems with definitions that have needed updating and 'new' forms of bodily injury. In trying to keep the OAPA relevant, have judges gone too far in their interpretation of this elderly statute?

Do you think it should be a criminal offence – subject to six months imprisonment – to cause a person to 'apprehend violence' or to touch someone in a way that may be unwanted but which causes no physical harm? Do you think the public perception of 'assault' and 'battery' are in line with the legal definitions of these offences?

With society's more relaxed attitudes to an individual's private life, should a person be able to consent to a level of harm for the purposes of sexual satisfaction? It may be seen by some to be less harmful or distressing than some forms of 'intimate piercings' which are allowed by the law. Is this prohibition simply a form of prejudice rather than a genuine public requirement?

FURTHER READING

Bell, B and Harrison, K, 'ABH and GBH in the House of Lords' (1992) 142 NLJ 166 – a discussion and critique on the *mens rea* of s 47 OATPA after the cases of *Savage* and *Parmenter*.

Clarkson, C, 'Law Commission's Report on OAP' [1994] Crim LR 324 – A look at the inconsistencies in the law in this area and the Law Commissions proposals for simplifying the offences against the person.

Weait, M, 'Knowledge, Autonomy and Consent: R v Konzani' [2005] Crim LR 763–72 – an article about the reckless transmission of HIV following the case of *Konzani*.

Leng, R, 'Consent and Offences against the Person: Law Commission Consultation Paper No.134' [1994] Crim LR 480–88 – an interesting and informative article focussing on the issue of consent to injury from different perspectives.

COMPANION WEBSITE

An online glossary compiled by the authors is available on the companion website: www.routledge.com/cw/beginningthelaw

Chapter 8
Rape

LEARNING OBJECTIVES

By the end of the chapter you should be able to:

- Understand the background to the enactment of the Sexual Offences Act 2003
- Appreciate the modernisation of the law in the recent legislation
- Understand the problems that arise in respect of the issue of consent in sexual offences generally
- Be aware of the problems that are still relevant with regards to consent to sexual activity

INTRODUCTION

Rape is a difficult crime to investigate and prosecute, as it often occurs when only the potential defendant and victim are present, and it is the word of one person against another, in a situation where there is likely to be acute distress. Although law enforcement are now much more sensitive about some issues, it is a fact that some people do 'cry rape' and it is a very serious and horrific crime even to be questioned about. A man could find his reputation and livelihood ruined after a charge, even if he is completely exonerated.

Sexual offences in England and Wales were overhauled recently, following a Law Commission Report (*Setting the Boundaries: Reforming the Law on Sex Offences* (2000)) which called the previous law, which was covered by the Sexual Offences Act 1957 '[a]rchaic, incoherent and discriminatory'.

This led to the Government of the day publishing a White Paper – *Protecting the Public* (2002) and this in turn led to the Sexual Offences Act 2003.

The main offence discussed in this chapter will be the offence of rape under s 1(1) of the Sexual Offences Act (SOA) 2003.

A person (A) commits an offence if:

(a)   he intentionally penetrates the vagina, anus or mouth of another person (B) with his penis

(b) B does not consent to the penetration, and

(c) A does not reasonably believe that B consents.

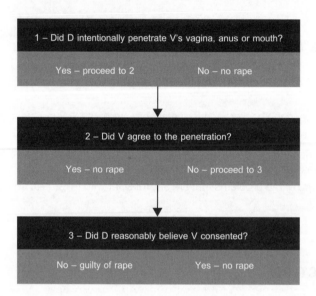

From this it is possible to create a breakdown of the elements of the offence as in the table below. Note that s 1(1) of the SOA 2003 is gender neutral in that it uses initials instead of personal pronouns, except for the defendant in s 1(1)a.

Actus reus	*Mens rea*
Penetration of vagina, mouth or anus of V	Intention to penetrate
Penetration must be with D's penis	D must have no reasonable belief in V's consent
Penetration must be without V's consent	

From these elements it is important to note that the issue of consent is relevant to BOTH the *actus reus* and the *mens rea* of the offence.

ACTUS REUS

Penetration

Under the Sexual Offences Act 1956, s 1, 'It is a felony for a man to rape a woman.'

This old law (now repealed) made it clear that only vaginal penetration was to be called rape. Other offences covered the acts of anal and oral penetration without consent. These meant that it was impossible to 'rape' a man and a defendant could only be charged with 'sexual assault'. It was felt increasingly that this was discriminatory and forcing a man to have sex should be seen and labelled by the law as seriously as the offence of forcing a woman to have sex.

The Criminal Justice and Public Order Act 1994 amended the SOA 1956 to recognise anal rape as an equal offence with vaginal rape, whether with a man or a woman.

The SOA 2003 also includes oral penetration as the *actus reus* of rape.

Section 79 of the SOA 2003 gives a definition of the sexual organs and makes it clear that the 'slightest penetration' is sufficient for rape to have taken place, there is no need for the man to have fully entered the victim, or ejaculated.

Penetration is defined as 'a continuing act from entry to withdrawal' (s 79(2)).

KEY CASE: *Kaitamaki* [1985] AC 147

Facts:

- The V and the D began to have sex.
- At some point the V decided that she wanted to stop having intercourse, and told the D to stop.
- The D did not stop and continued to have sex with the V.
- The D was charged with rape even though the initial penetration was consensual.

Held:

It was held that penetration was a 'continuing act' and once consent was removed the *actus reus* of rape was complete if the D did not withdraw.

Penis

Rape can only be committed by a male, as only men have a penis. After the SOA 2003 the penis can be one that is surgically constructed, as may be the case in a female to male transsexual.

A woman can be an accessory to rape as in the case of *DPP v K and B* (1997) 1 Cr App R 36. In this case two girls lured another girl to a place where they encouraged a boy to have sex with her against her will. Although the boy was not found, the girls were charged with being accessories to rape (see Chapter 10). They were liable to the same maximum sentence as if they had committed the offence – potentially life imprisonment for rape.

Without consent

Consent is an important part of both the *actus reus* and the *mens rea* of the offence of rape. As part of the *actus reus* it is the only thing that separates a loving act of sexual intercourse from a serious offence. Consent will be dealt with later on in the chapter.

MENS REA

Intentional penetration

It is difficult to imagine when a man could penetrate the mouth, vagina or anus of another with his penis without intention to do so. An example could be given however if a man was so intoxicated that they were incapable of forming the necessary intention. Remember the *Majewski* rule? Intoxication is not a defence but can negate the defendant's intention. The *Majewski* rule would usually then find the defendant reckless of a lesser offence, but under the SOA 2003 there is no offence of reckless penetration.

No reasonable belief in consent

This element consists of asking two questions:

1.   Did the defendant believe the victim was consenting? If no, then there was no belief – this is a subjective test.
2.   Was that belief reasonable? If no, there is no reasonable belief – this is an objective test (remember that the jury are the 'reasonable man').

Section 1(2) of the SOA 2003 states – 'Whether a belief is reasonable is to be determined having regard to all the circumstances, including any steps A has taken to ascertain whether B consents.'

Another welcome reform in the area of sexual offences made by the SOA 2003 is the move away from 'honest belief' in the victim's consent, to 'reasonable belief'. Previously, if a defendant really believed he had the other person's consent to sex, no matter how unreasonable that belief, he could not be convicted.

Consider the case of *DPP v Morgan* [1976] AC 182.

KEY CASE: *DPP v Morgan* [1976] AC 182

Facts:

- Mr Morgan invited three colleagues back to his house to have sex with his wife.
- He told them that she had a 'rape fantasy' and if she screamed and protested they were to ignore her as she would only be 'acting the part'.
- He gave the three men condoms and they went with him and had sex with Mrs Morgan, in spite of her distress and pleas for them to stop.
- All three were charged with rape and Mr Morgan was charged with aiding and abetting rape (until 1991 and the case of *R v R* [1991] 3 WLR 767 a husband could not be charged with the rape of his wife).
- The three men said they honestly believed that the wife was consenting on the grounds of what Mr Morgan had told them.

Held:

The House of Lords (now the Supreme Court) held that it was the defendant's **honest belief** that was important, and not whether that belief was reasonable.

In the case of *Morgan* however, the convictions were upheld. The court decided that no one could have maintained such an honest belief in the face of Mrs Morgan's distress.

In spite of the outcome, the precedent of honest belief was troubling and unwelcome. The SOA 2003 clarifies and codifies the concept of reasonable belief.

CONSENT

The triumph of the SOA 2003, and the way in which it really reforms the law is how the statute deals with consent. Section 74 defines consent, s 75 gives **rebuttable** (evidential) presumptions about whether consent exists, and s 76 gives two situations which form **irrebuttable** (conclusive) presumptions that consent is not present.

Section 76 brings case law under the statutory umbrella. This is not new law, but it codifies case law that has formed part of the common law development of the SOA 1956. It is helpful to look at the provision backwards, starting with where the presumption arises and going on to look at what the presumption is. Section 76(2) states:

> The circumstances (where the presumption arises) are that:
>
> (a)   the defendant intentionally deceived the complainant as to the nature or purpose of the relevant act;
>
> (b)   the defendant intentionally induced the complainant to consent to the relevant act by impersonating a person known personally to the complainant.

Part (a) covers the case of *Flattery* (1877) 2 QBD 410 – note the age of the case and the difference in the girl's awareness here. In this case, a girl was told that she needed an operation to improve her health. The defendant had sex with the girl, but she was not aware that was what he was doing. When charged with rape, the defendant said the girl had consented. The Court held she had been deceived as to the nature or purpose of the act which took place. She had agreed to the 'operation' not to sexual intercourse.

Part (b) covers the case of *Elbekkay* [1995] Crim LR 163, CA. In this case, a man, his girlfriend and a male friend had been out together and had gone back to the couple's home. They watched television for a while and then the girlfriend went to bed. The man (her partner) fell asleep on the sofa in front of the television and his male friend then went into the bedroom and began to have sex with the girlfriend, allowing her to believe he was her partner. When she realised who it was she pushed him away.

For part (b) to be successful, the defendant must know that he is being mistaken for someone else, and the mistake must be about someone who is personally known to the victim. If a man tells a woman he is a Premiership footballer to get her to sleep with him, there is no offence – the woman knows who she is agreeing to have sex with, even if he does not have the job or status that she believes he has!

If either of these two situations arise, it is to be conclusively presumed under s 76(1):

> (a)   that the complainant did not consent to the relevant act, and
>
> (b)   that the defendant did not believe that the complainant consented to the relevant act.

This means that the prosecution do not have to prove those two elements of the offence (the *mens rea* elements) and have only to prove intentional penetration took place.

Section 75

This section contains the rebuttable or evidential presumptions. We will look at when these presumptions arise, and then what the presumptions are. There are six situations covered by s 75(2):

The circumstances are that:

(a)   any person was, at the time of the relevant act or immediately before it began, using violence against the complainant or causing the complainant to fear that immediate violence would be used against him;

(b)   any person was, at the time of the relevant act or immediately before it began, causing the complainant to fear that violence was being used, or that immediate violence would be used, against another person;

(c)   the complainant was, and the defendant was not, unlawfully detained at the time of the relevant act;

(d)   the complainant was asleep or otherwise unconscious at the time of the relevant act;

(e)   because of the complainant's physical disability, the complainant would not have been able at the time of the relevant act to communicate to the defendant whether the complainant consented;

(f)   any person had administered to or caused to be taken by the complainant, without the complainant's consent, a substance which, having regard to when it was administered or taken, was capable of causing or enabling the complainant to be stupefied or overpowered at the time of the relevant act.

Some of these presumptions may seem puzzling. It may seem relevant to ask why the threat of violence against an individual or a third person – such as the victim's child – is not a conclusive presumption. It might be suggested that the use of violence in sexual intercourse (as covered by section (a)) is not always indicative of lack of consent. A person may welcome it. It is less easy to argue why the threat of violence against a third person should ever be rebuttable, however – as covered by (b). It is also interesting to note the use of the word 'fear' in s 75. This appears to be a less flexible word than 'apprehension' as used in the Offences Against the Person Act 1861 (see Chapter 7). If someone consents to intercourse because of genuine fear of violence, it is difficult to see what evidence could be presented by the defence to rebut this.

Subsection (c) might raise the same concerns. It has been suggested that such a situation may arise where a captive falls in love with his or her captor, but if an individual is unlawfully detained and the defendant is not, it may stretch credibility to say that intercourse was freely consented to.

Subsection (d) covers a presumption which used to be **irrebutable** (conclusive) before the SOA 2003 came into force and could be said to have relaxed the law in this situation. Again, it is difficult to imagine how someone could have given their consent to sexual intercourse when they are asleep or unconscious – common sense would tell a person that consent here is simply not possible. This section, together with s 75(2)(f) (below) has also highlighted concerns about consent after the consumption of alcohol.

Subsection (e) is clearly designed to be protective of the vulnerable in society, but criticisms can be made of this section also. It appears to cover only physical disabilities, and it demands communication of consent to the defendant, which none of the other sections seem to do. It must be assumed that this cannot be confined to speech, as it is easy to imagine a person communicating their willingness for sexual intercourse by other means.

Subsection (f) could apply in cases where a person has a 'date rape' drug slipped into a drink, or simply when a person has drunk too much alcohol. The question of alcohol intoxication is a serious one and one that the SOA 2003 does not really get to grips with. When the Bill was going through Parliament, the Home Secretary at the time – David Blunkett – proposed that there should be an irrebuttable presumption where the victim was very drunk. It was decided however, that such a clause would be too complicated to draw up as there can be no identification of when an individual would be 'too drunk' to consent. In the case of *Malone* (1998) 2 Cr App R 447 a man had sex with a 16-year-old girl who was so drunk that she was passing in and out of consciousness. He was convicted of rape.

Note that the substance given in subsection (f) only has to be 'capable' of causing the stupification, and can be given to the victim by anyone, not just the defendant.

If anyone of these six situations occurs and the defendant knows it has occurred, s 75(1) states that the following is to be assumed:

> the complainant is to be taken not to have consented to the relevant act unless sufficient evidence is adduced to raise an issue as to whether he consented, and the defendant is to be taken not to have reasonably believed that the complainant consented unless sufficient evidence is adduced to raise an issue as to whether he reasonably believed it.

It can be seen from this that these presumptions are only a starting point, and the defendant can present evidence to rebut them.

Example

Rick meets Jenny in a club. They both have a lot to drink and leave together in a taxi which takes them back to Jenny's flat. The next morning Jenny reports that she has been raped. If she had drunk a lot of alcohol, the presumption under s 75(2)(f) would be that she had not consented and Rick did not reasonably believe she had consented. However, Rick only has to present evidence to rebut this presumption. This might be that the two of them indulged in heavy petting in the taxi. Faced with this, the burden falls back on to the prosecution to prove Jenny's lack of consent and that Rick had no reasonable belief in her consent to the criminal standard of proof, which is 'beyond reasonable doubt'.

---

s 74

Section 74 provides a definition of 'consent'. This can be used by the jury when s 76 and s 75 are not applicable.

Section 74 states simply:

> For the purposes of this Part, a person consents if he agrees by choice, and has the freedom and capacity to make that choice.

It is obvious that this is not a perfect definition, but it is the first time an English statute has attempted to define consent for the purpose of sexual offences. Although we are discussing rape under s 1(1) of the SOA 2003, the presumptions under ss 76 and 75 and the defintion of consent under s 74 are applicable across the whole of the Act.

There can be little problem with the idea of agreement by choice, but the language is less clear when it comes to 'freedom and capacity'.

On-the-spot question

? Consider these facts: Sophie is homeless, cold and hungry. As she walks along the street one night a car pulls up beside her and a man offers her money for sex. Sophie accepts, knowing she will be able to afford to buy a warm coat and some hot meals with the money.

It seems that Sophie has consented to sex in this situation, but can she be said to have the freedom and capacity to make that choice? Even if she has, can the same be said of a person desperate for alcohol or drugs because of an addiction?

KEY CASE: *Olugboja* **[1982] 1 WLR 1382**

Facts:

- Two women met two men on a night out.
- The men offered the women a lift home, but drove instead to the men's flat.
- Once there, each of the men raped one of the women.
- When they had finished they 'swapped' women and one of the men took one of the women into the bedroom.
- He said to her, 'Take off your trousers, I am going to have sex with you.'
- The woman did as he asked and did not resist as he had intercourse with her.
- When he was charged with her rape, he claimed she consented to the sex.

Held:

In considering the appeal against conviction, the Court of Appeal said, 'Genuine consent covers a wide range of states of mind, from desire to reluctant aquiescence.'

However, submission by fear or apathy could not be called consent, and where there was fear, as in this case, it was ridiculous to say that the victim consented.

A further problem is one raised earlier under s 75 – the issue of when a person is so intoxicated that they claim not to have consented to sex. In the case of *Bree* [2007] EWCA Crim 804, a woman claimed she had been raped. The man admitted to having sex with her. They were both very drunk and he had walked her home. He claimed the sex was consensual. The Court of Appeal held that if the woman had the capacity to consent, even her drunken consent was sufficient, but when she was so intoxicated that she had lost her capacity to choose to have sex, she could not be said to be consenting. As the level of drunkeness and ability to consent would vary from person to person and even from day to day, such cases had to be decided very much on the facts of the individual case.

On-the-spot question

Jon is married to Debbie. Jon threatens to slap their three-year-old daughter if Debbie does not have sex with him. Frightened, Debbie agrees. Is Jon guilty of rape? (Tip – Consider s 76, then s 75 and then s 74.)

SUMMARY

The 2003 Act brought much needed reform to the law of sexual offences in England and Wales.

- The definition of rape under s 1(1) is now gender neutral and includes non-consensual penetration of the mouth.
- The Act also defines consent for the first time under s 74, and assists juries further with the irrebuttable presumptions under s 76 and the rebuttable presumptions under s 75.
- The Act has also codified case law such as *Kaitamaki* and *Elbekkay* which ensures these precendents cannot be overturned.
- One of the *mens rea* elements is now a lack of 'reasonable belief' in the victim's consent. This replaces 'honest belief' from the case of *Morgan.*
- While there is much good to be said about the Act, there are also some criticisms. The problem of consent when intoxicated is still very much in debate.

KEY CASES

Case	Legal principle
Kaitamaki (1985)	Penetration is a continuing act from entry to withdrawal
Flattery (1877)	There is no consent when the victim is deceived as to the nature and purpose of the act
Elbekkay (1995)	There is no consent when the victim is deceived by the impersonation of someone known personally to them
Olugboja (1982)	Submission is not consent
Bree (2007)	Drunken consent is still consent if victim has the capacity to make a choice.

ISSUES TO THINK ABOUT FURTHER

The SOA 2003 has brought some changes to the law, but has it gone far enough? The number of rape convictions is a tiny minority of the number of rapes charged, and the number of rapes charged is a tiny minority of the number of rapes that are estimated to happen to men and women every year.

The cases of 'stranger rape' may be clear cut, but most non-consensual sexual intercourse takes place between people who already know each other, and juries may be hesitant to convict a man for such a serious crime simply on the word of another person, especially if that person – or both parties – were intoxicated.

The victims in rape cases are automatically granted anonymity during the trial and afterwards, but this is not given to the man accused. Some individuals may 'cry rape' in revenge, or because an infidelity would otherwise be exposed, but even if he is exonerated completely, the man will continue to be associated with the charge and may lose his family, job or friends because of it. It may be time to extend the idea of anonymity to both parties, and only reveal the name of the accused if he is found guilty.

FURTHER READING

Elvin, J, 'The Concept of Consent under the Sexual Offences Act 2003' (2008) Journal of Criminal Law 72 (519) – an article on the main concept of consent and suggestions for further reform of the law in this area.

Finch, E and Munro, V, 'Intoxicated consent and the boundaries of drug assisted rape' [2003] Crim LR 773–87 – a detailed investigation into intoxicated consent and the validity of such consent.

R v McAllister [1997] Crim LR 233 – a short case comment about the difficult line between consent, reluctant aquiesence and submission.

R v R [1991] 2 All ER 257 – this is the case that changed the law so that a husband could be convicted of raping his wife.

COMPANION WEBSITE

An online glossary compiled by the authors is available on the companion website: www.routledge.com/cw/beginningthelaw

Chapter 9
Theft

LEARNING OBJECTIVES

By the end of the chapter you should be able to:

- Appreciate that theft is an offence against property
- Be aware that it is a statutory offence under s 1 of the Theft Act 1968
- Know the three *actus reus* elements and two *mens rea* elements
- Appreciate that all five elements must be present for a conviction
- Be aware of the problems with the definition of dishonesty in the Theft Act 1968

INTRODUCTION

Theft is an offence against property. The owner of the property has an absolute right to do what he wants to with it; whether it's to keep it, destroy it or give it away. Theft interferes with that right. Theft is an offence which can be tried either at the magistrates' court or at the Crown Court, depending on the value of the property stolen, and is subject to a maximum term of imprisonment of seven years if heard at the Crown Court. It is a statutory offence and is defined by s 1 of the Theft Act 1968. The Theft Act 1968 replaced the Larceny Act 1916 which had become cluttered with dense language and technical offences which were difficult to understand, even for prosecutors and lawyers. By contrast, the Theft Act 1968 was supposed to be a model of clarity, using words that jurors would easily be able to interpret. This aspiration on the part of the drafters of the Theft Act has not proved to be entirely true.

Statutory crimes are relatively straightforward to learn and apply to problem scenarios as all the relevant information is contained within the statute itself. Case law is also needed, however, to illustrate the definitions of key words in the Theft Act.

Almost all criminal offences can be broken down into *actus reus* and *mens rea* requirements (see Chapters 2 and 3 for definitions) and theft is no exception. The *actus reus* and *mens rea* can be found within the definition in s 1.

Key Definition

Section 1(1) of the Theft Act 1968: a person is guilty of theft if he dishonestly appropriates property belonging to another with the intention of permanently depriving the other of it; and 'thief' and 'steal' shall be construed accordingly.

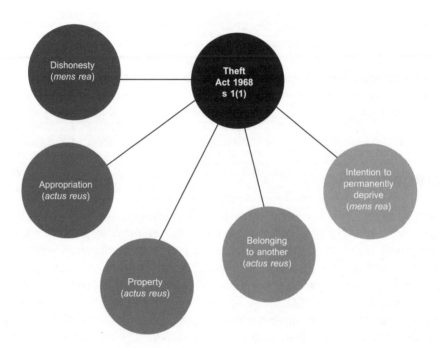

These five elements are the essential components of the theft offence. The offence cannot be charged if all five are not present at the same time, as held in the case of *Lawrence v Metropolitan Police Commissioner* [1972] AC 626. Once the five coincide, theft is complete.

Example

Jane goes into a shop intending to steal, and picks up a lipstick to put into her bag without paying. At this point – as you will see – all five elements above are present and theft is complete. If Jane then decides to pay for the lipstick she will obviously not be charged with theft as there is no proof of her dishonesty, but in theory, the theft has already occurred.

Remember – a question in an exam will not require you second guess a jury's decision, you can only apply the sections of the statute as they have been interpreted by the courts. This means you need to know case law in order to give authority to your answers.

IS THE *ACTUS REUS* PRESENT?

The *actus reus* of theft is:

- **Appropriation**
- Of property
- Belonging to another.

All three of these elements must be present for the *actus reus* to be complete. If one is missing, there can be no *actus reus* and therefore no offence of theft.

Appropriation

When the Theft Act was drafted, it was thought that appropriation was a word that juries would easily understand and needed no further clarification. We shall see just how wrong this turned out to be.

Section 3(1) of the Theft Act 1968 reads:

> Any assumption by a person of the rights of the owner amounts to an appropriation, and this includes, where he has come by the property (innocently or not), without stealing it, any later assumption of a right to it by keeping or dealing with it as owner.

This has been interpreted very widely. In the case of *Morris* [1983] AC 182, the Court held that it was only necessary for the defendant (D) to assume one of the rights of the owner. The D had swapped price labels on goods in a supermarket in order to obtain an item at a cheaper price. It was held that pricing the item was a right of the owner and it was sufficient for appropriation that the D had assumed that right.

Appropriation and consent

A real issue for the courts has been whether or not the victim's consent to the goods being taken is fatal to a charge of theft. In the *Lawrence* case a taxi driver took too much money from his customer's proffered wallet. He argued there could be no appropriation as the customer had consented to the money being taken. The court held that consent is immaterial to appropriation and found the taxi driver guilty of theft.

This was confirmed in the leading case of *DPP v Gomez* [1992] 3 WLR 1061, in which the Court confirmed the legal principle formulated in *Lawrence* that the owner's consent is irrelevant to the question of appropriation.

KEY CASE: *DPP v Gomez* [1992] 3 WLR 1061

Facts:

- The first defendant (D1) wanted to use fraudulently obtained cheques to obtain goods.
- The second defendant (D2) worked at a store where D1 presented the cheques as payment.
- The manager of the store asked D2 to verify the authenticity of the cheques, D2 only pretended to ring the bank concerned and told the manager he had been cleared to accept them.
- The manager then agreed to D1 taking the goods.
- When charged with theft D1 and D2 argued that the manager of the shop consented to the goods being taken – as he believed the cheques to be genuine.

Held:

The court held there had been an appropriation (and therefore theft) of the goods.

It might be noted that theft was an odd choice of charge for this action. It may have been more appropriate to charge the D's with 'obtaining property by deception' under what was s 15 of the Theft Act (TA) 1968 (note, this section of the TA 1968 has since been repealed by the Fraud Act 2006).

The two cases of *Lawrence* and *Gomez* are of particular importance as they illustrate how wide the definition of appropriation has become. The courts have interpreted this word in s 3 of the TA 1968 to have a completely neutral connotation.

On-the-spot question

 Jamil asks to borrow a friend's textbook to look up a case. The friend agrees and Jamil picks up the book and opens it. Has Jamil appropriated the book?

Appropriation and gifts

The case of *Mazo* (1997) 2 Cr App R 518 initially indicated that a valid *inter vivos* (during a person's lifetime) gift could not be charged as theft as there would be no appropriation. A gift might not be valid however, if the giver is not held to be mentally capable of disposing of their property. In *Hinks* [2001] 2 AC 241, a man with a very low IQ gave gifts of a television set and sums of money totalling over £60,000 to a woman friend. The court held he was capable of giving a valid gift, but such a gift could still amount to an appropriation of the property. If the other four elements were present, the jury could convict the defendant of theft.

This may be problematic. As has already been said it is the right of an owner to give his property away and this seems to be at odds with the judgment in *Hinks*. Also, under civil law, the property passes to the receiver of the gift at the time of the giving. It is then difficult to see how the property can be deemed to 'belong to another' as required under TA 1968, s 5 (see below). It is undesirable for civil and criminal law to be so out of step. A person could be convicted of theft, but could not be made to return the property gifted. This seems to be a confusing and unsatisfactory state for the law to be in.

On-the-spot question

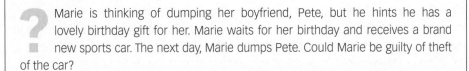 Marie is thinking of dumping her boyfriend, Pete, but he hints he has a lovely birthday gift for her. Marie waits for her birthday and receives a brand new sports car. The next day, Marie dumps Pete. Could Marie be guilty of theft of the car?

Property

Property is defined in s 4 of the Theft Act 1968. The thing that is appropriated must be property otherwise there can be no theft.

Section 4(1) of the Theft Act 1968 reads:

> Property includes money and all other property, real or personal, including things in action and other intangible property.

Section 4 refers to 'real property'. This means *freehold land*. 'Personal property' under s 4 relates to items an individual would own, such as a car, jewellery, or a book. A thing in action, sometimes still referred to as a 'chose in action' is something such as a credit in a bank account or shares in a company. All of these things are capable of being stolen.

Section 4 gives a very wide definition of property and case law tends to be used to give examples of what is *not* property, such as confidential information in the case of *Oxford and Moss* (1979) 68 Cr App R 183.

KEY CASE: *Oxford and Moss* **(1979) 68 Cr App R 183**

Facts:

- A university student took an exam paper from a tutor's desk, copied it and replaced the paper.
- It was held he could not be charged with theft as the information on the exam paper was not property.

Held:

It was held by the Court that information such as this is not property. Had the student taken the exam paper and kept it, he could have been charged with theft of the paper, which is **tangible** property.

A corpse or parts of it are also not property. Such an item can only be classified as 'property' – and so be stolen – if it was subject to the application of human skill such as to reduce it into possession. In *Doodwarde v Spence* (1908) 6 CLR 406, a malformed foetus displayed in a 'freak show' (note the year) was held to be in the lawful possession of an individual because it had been preserved in a jar of formaldehyde. Other items that are not property are listed in s 4(4), such as wild animals and wild growing plants and mushrooms.

On-the-spot question

? Sara, a medical student, is dissecting a corpse that has been donated to her teaching hospital. In order to work on it further, she removes the preserved foot from the corpse and takes it home with her. Could Sara be charged with theft of the foot?

Belonging to another

The property which has been appropriated must belong to another. This is defined in s 5 of the TA 1968 as someone 'in possession or control' of the property. It is easy to see that this is a wider definition than one based on the 'ordinary' meaning of belonging to another.

> ### Example
>
> Karen hires a bike from Saul, and pays him £30 for a week. After 5 days Saul takes the bike back without Karen's knowledge because another person wants to hire it. Although we might say the bike 'belongs' to Saul, it is in the possession and control of Karen for the whole week. It is therefore possible that Saul has 'stolen' his own bike – subject to the other elements of theft being present.

In the case of *Turner (No 2)* [1971] 2 All ER 441, a man sent his car to a garage for repair and then took it from the garage forecourt at night without paying the bill. He argued that he could not be guilty of theft of the car as it didn't belong to another (remember all five elements must be present for a guilty verdict). The court held that the car was in the possession and control of the garage until the bill had been paid.

Abandoned property

Sometimes a defendant may argue that he has taken property which has no owner and therefore does not 'belong to another'. An item of property is only abandoned if the former owner is completely disinterested in what becomes of it. A householder putting property in their rubbish bin has not abandoned it, the householder is signalling her intention that the local council remove the property and take it to the refuse tip. Once the property is in the possession and control of the council, it belongs to the council and if removed from the tip will be the appropriation of property belonging to another. The courts generally are unhappy with declaring property belongs to no-one and this makes sense in our society which is largely built on the defence of property rights. Consider the case of *Rostron* [2003] EWCA Crim 2206.

KEY CASE: *Rostron* [2003] EWCA Crim 2206

Facts:

- The defendant, dressed in scuba gear, retrieved golf balls from the bottom of a water hazard on a golf course.
- He was charged with theft of the balls.
- He argued that the balls did not 'belong to another' as their original owners no longer cared what had become of them.
- He was convicted of theft of the balls.

Held:

The court decided the balls belonged to the golf club as they took precautions – a security guard – to prevent trespassers on the private course.

Property obtained by mistake

If a person gets property by the mistake of another, then s 5(4) of the TA 1968 states that the property remains the property of the other and the person is under an obligation to return the property.

> **Example**
>
> Jerome buys a sandwich from the supermarket and pays with a £5 note. The cashier gives him change for a £10 note. Jerome notices, but decides not to say anything. Jerome has appropriated property belonging to another. If the *mens rea* of theft is also present he will be guilty of theft.

Property given for a purpose

Section 5(3) of the Theft Act 1968 states:

> Where a person receives property from or on account of another, and is under an obligation to retain and deal with that property or its proceeds in a particular way, the property or proceeds shall be regarded (as against him) as belonging to the other.

In the case of *Davidge v Bunnett* [1984] Crim LR 297, V had given money to a flatmate to pay a share of the gas bill. The flatmate spent the money and argued, that while he certainly owed V the money, he had not stolen it, as once given to him, the money was not property belonging to another. It was accepted that he would not have paid the bill with the exact notes and coins the V had given him – see *Velumyl*, below. It was held that D had a duty arising out of s 5(3) even though he may have been the legal owner of the money. It has been held that the obligation arising in s 5(3) must be a legal obligation, not merely a social or moral obligation.

In *Lewis v Lethbridge* [1987] Crim LR 59, DC, D raised sponsorship money for a charity. Although his sponsors paid him, he did not pass the money on to the charity in question. In this case, the D was not convicted of theft because there was no legal obligation to deal with the money in a particular way – although there was clearly a moral obligation to hand the money over. D did, however, owe a **civil debt** to the charity.

It can be seen that it is easy to commit the *actus reus* of theft. Everyone appropriates property belonging to another every day. Picking up a packet of biscuits in the supermarket, borrowing a friend's pen, even unwrapping your own birthday present! Thanks to the neutral meaning now ascribed to appropriation and the very wide definition given to both 'property' and 'belonging to another', it is rare to find the jury troubled by the *actus reus* of the crime. In order to distinguish between the innocent majority and the genuine thief, it is necessary to give very close attention to the *mens rea* of the offence.

IS THE *MENS REA* PRESENT?

The *mens rea* of theft is:

- Dishonesty.
- Intention to permanently deprive.

Dishonesty

Dishonesty is a fundamental concept to the whole law of theft and exam questions will frequently focus on this aspect of the law. Often a person's guilt or innocence will depend on the jury's view of the persons honesty, or otherwise. Dishonesty has only a negative definition under the TA 1968. Section 2 gives three situations when the defendant will be held not to be dishonest.

Section 2(1)(a) – where the D honestly believes he has the right in law to appropriate the property on behalf of himself or another.

Example

In the case of *Skivington* [1968] 1 QB 166, CA a man assaulted a clerk and demanded his wife's wages – which he thought she was owed. This was not theft as the man believed he had the right in law to demand the wages.

Section 2(1)(b) – where the D honestly believes he would have the consent of the owner had the owner known of the circumstances of the appropriation.

> **Example**
>
> Pat takes a bottle of milk from her neighbour's step, meaning to replace it later in the day when she goes to the shops. Pat is sure her neighbour, who is a good friend, will not mind.

Section 2(1)(c) – where the D honestly believes he could not find the owner of the property by taking reasonable steps.

> **Example**
>
> Sree finds a ten pound note in an empty field. There is no-one around and she decides to keep the money.

In all of these circumstances the belief of the D needs to be honestly held, but the belief need not be objectively reasonable. It is a subjective concept. However, in s 2(1)(c), the steps considered to find the owner of the property must be reasonable. Note that the steps do not have to be actually taken, or attempted. What is reasonable will depend on what the property is.

> **Example**
>
> Sree finds a bag containing £10,000 in an empty field. There is no-one around and she decides to keep the money.

Here the jury may feel that it would be reasonable of Sree to contact the police and hand such a large sum of money in, given that someone is likely to have reported the loss or theft of it. By keeping the money, Sree may be found to be dishonest.

Outside of these limited circumstances, the TA 1968 gives no help to the jury on the question of dishonesty. It has been left to case law to further define the concept and provide a test to be applied when the issue of honesty is in doubt. The positive definition of dishonesty was formulated by two cases, the cases of *Feely* and *Ghosh*.

In *Feely* [1973] 1 All ER 341, a worker in a shop borrowed money from his employer's till in spite of being warned it would not be tolerated. He said he always meant to repay the money on pay day, and indeed he had left an IOU in the till. He was found guilty of theft. The judge considered that the jury would know what dishonesty was and told them:

> Jurors . . . should apply the current standards of ordinary decent people. In their own lives they have to decide what is and what is not dishonest. We can see no reason why, when in a jury box, they should require the help of a judge to tell then what amounts to dishonesty.

It can be seen that this is an objective view. Mr Feely was judged on what 'ordinary decent people' considered dishonest, even if he genuinely saw nothing wrong with his conduct. A further problem is that this test assumes there is a standard of 'ordinary decent people' who would agree on a standard of dishonesty. This is plainly not the case. What the public see as dishonest varies with time, with culture and the demographic of the section of the public polled. This may allow an uncomfortable uncertainty into the law of theft and mean that cases with similar facts may not be decided alike.

The case of *R v Ghosh* [1982] QB 1053 is now the leading case in this area. The *Ghosh* test added an extra question to the *Feely* test.

The jury should be asked:

1. Was the action dishonest according to the ordinary standards of reasonable and honest people?
2. Did the defendant realise that reasonable and honest people would regard what he did as dishonest?

The answer to both these questions must be 'yes' for the defendant to be dishonest.

Ghosh was a doctor who argued with his hospital about money he was owed for an operation. He submitted false documents implying he had undertaken another operation for which he claimed the amount he was owed. Ghosh said this was his money anyway and he was not dishonest. The jury were asked to apply the two-stage test above and he was found guilty of obtaining by deception under what was then s 15 of the TA 1968 (this section has since been repealed). The test however, is relevant to *all* statutory definitions of dishonesty.

Although this test for dishonesty still relies on the standards of 'reasonable honest people', it can be seen to be much more balanced than the purely objective *Feely* test. The *Ghosh* test depends on the defendant subjectively realising his conduct was dishonest. This genuinely attempts to reveal the defendant's state of mind, which is the *mens rea* of the crime.

Intention to permanently deprive

Under common law and under the Larceny Act 1916, there could be no theft of property if it was the intention of the D to return it. This rule is preserved in the TA 1968.

> ### Example
>
> Joe takes a clean coffee mug from Pat's desk drawer and uses it to make coffee. Pat is annoyed and upset that she cannot find the mug, but Joe says nothing. Several days later he washes and returns the mug. This is not theft, as Joe had no intention depriving Pat permanently of her property, even though it seems likely he has committed the other four elements required.

Intention to permanently deprive is defined under s 6 of the TA 1968. Again the definition given is very much wider than an ordinary, everyday definition of such a phrase.

> s 6(1) – A person appropriating property belonging to another without meaning the other permanently to lose the thing itself is nevertheless to be regarded as having the intention of permanently depriving the other of it if his intention is to treat the thing as his own to dispose of regardless of the other's rights; and a borrowing or lending of it may amount to so treating it if, but only if, the borrowing or lending is for a period and in circumstances making it equivalent to an outright taking or disposal.

At first sight this looks like a complicated section, and it is best thought of in two parts. A D will be deemed to have the intention to permanently deprive if there is:

- an intention to treat the property as his own to dispose of regardless of the other's rights;
- a borrowing or lending is for a period or in a circumstance making it equivalent to an outright taking or disposal.

Intention

Intention has the same definition as was seen in the chapter on *mens rea*. Where a D maintains that he did not have a direct intention for a particular event to occur, the jury will be directed to ask themselves the two questions in the *Nedrick/Woollin* test.

- Was the outcome a virtually certain consequence of the defendant's action?
- If so, was the defendant aware of this?

Permanently deprive

If someone takes another's sandwich and eats it, there is clearly an intention to permanently deprive as the property cannot be returned. However, what is to stop a person, caught with another's goods, merely stating that they intended to return the thing and were only 'borrowing' it? There have been difficulties with cases of a D taking a car and then abandoning it after driving home. Here there is no intention to permanently deprive, the D may have only been in the car for half an hour or less. A specific offence to cover this scenario is found in s 12 of the TA 1968, 'taking without owners consent' (TWOC). In other circumstances we must look more closely at the two parts of s 6(1).

Part one

The crucial question in this part has been the definition of the phrase 'dispose of'. It might be thought that this means to get rid of in some way, but again the courts have been very generous in their interpretation of the words of the statute. In the case of *Lavender* [1994] Crim LR 297, a council tenant removed doors from an empty council property which was being renovated and put them in his own (council owned) property. The tenant was convicted of theft of the doors because he treated them as his own – moving them and using them for his own purposes. It would be quite difficult in ordinary language to say he had 'disposed of' the doors, but the court held that 'dispose of' could mean no more than 'deal with'. Again, this is an uncomfortable interpretation of the Theft Act, as the D in *Lavender* seemed to be treating the doors as belonging to the council when he affixed them to the council property, rather than treating them as his own, regardless of the council's rights.

Part two

This part is intended to cover the situation where a D may technically be returning the item, but its value to the owner is lessened or destroyed.

Example

Peta takes Rupa's ticket for a West End show. After watching the show, Peta returns the ticket.

Without the second part of s 6, this could not be theft as Peta has not intended to permanently deprive Rupa of the cardboard ticket. She has, however, deprived her of the value that the ticket held, her right to be admitted to the theatre. In this scenario all the value has gone from the goods, but it is easy to imagine a situation where only part of the value has gone.

In the case of *Lloyd* [1985] QB 829 a D took film reels from a cinema where he worked and – in league with others – made copies of the films for the 'pirate' market. The film reels were then returned. The court held that there had been no theft as there was no intention to permanently deprive the cinema owner and the reels still retained their 'goodness and value'.

Money

In the case of *Velumyl* [1989] Crim LR 299 it was held that a person could be convicted of theft of money even if they returned the same amount of money to the V. This is because the D would be unable to return exactly the same coins and notes as he had taken.

On-the-spot question

 P'eta takes an umbrella from a stand in a restaurant. She mistakenly thinks it is her umbrella, but in fact it is a similar one which belongs to Laura. When she realises her mistake, P'eta decides to keep the umbrella. Is P'eta guilty of theft?

SUMMARY

- Theft is defined under s 1 of the Theft Act 1968. Sections 2–6 then define the elements described in s 1.
- All five elements – three *actus reus* and two *mens rea* – are necessary for the crime to be proven.
- Case law is important as it has widened the definition of the elements of theft.
- Appropriation is defined in s 3, but case law has expanded this definition to effectively encompass doing anything at all to anyone else's property, even with permission.
- As a result of this, the definition of dishonesty is very important, but there is only a partial definition in s 2. The *Ghosh* test is used by the jury to decide the question of dishonesty at trial.

KEY CASES

Case	Legal principle
Lawrence/Gomez (1992)/(1997)	Consent is immaterial to the concept of appropriation
Turner (1971)	A D can – in some circumstances – be convicted of stealing his own property

Oxford and Moss (1979)	Information is not property capable of being stolen
Ghosh (1982)	A D will be dishonest under this test if his act is dishonest to the standard of ordinary people and the D knew this
Lavender (1994)	To 'dispose of' in s 6 means no more than 'deal with'

ISSUES TO THINK ABOUT FURTHER

You should now understand that the definition of appropriation in the Theft Act 1968 has made the *actus reus* of theft much too wide. It now covers the merest touching of another's property. Even validly given gifts can be theft if a jury decides the defendant was dishonest in accepting the gift.

It is also apparent that the common law definition of dishonesty in the *Feely/Ghosh* test is unacceptably vague. As the *actus reus* is so easy to commit, juries need to have a statutory definition of 'dishonest' to avoid confusion and ensure like cases are treated alike.

The definition of 'intention to permanently deprive' is also stretched beyond an everyday understanding of the phrase by the two parts of s 6 and the wide definition in *Lavender*. The case of *Lavender* defined 'dispose of' in s 6 as meaning 'to deal with'.

Far from being a model of clarity and precision as the drafters of the Theft Act 1968 had intended, the wide definitions given to the other elements of theft by case law have meant that a defendant's liability for theft often comes down to whether or not the jury decide he is 'dishonest'.

FURTHER READING

Shute, S, 'Appropriation and the law of theft' [2002] Crim LR 445–58 – an examination of the case of *Hinks* (2001) and support for the extension of theft to valid gifts.

Pawlowski, M, 'Dead bodies as property' (1996) 146 NLJ 1828–29 – the historical settings and precedent for the decision in *Dobson* (1996).

Halpin, A, 'The Test for Dishonesty' [1996] Crim LR 283–95 – an investigation into the *Ghosh* test and support for the judgment, with some ideas for a general definition of dishonesty.

Smith, JC, 'Current Topic, Stealing Tickets' [1998] Crim LR 723–27 – a short, but interesting article on whether buying a train ticket buys you just the right to travel, or the ticket as well.

COMPANION WEBSITE

An online glossary compiled by the authors is available on the companion website: www.routledge.com/cw/beginningthelaw

Chapter 10
Forms of liability – inchoate offences and joint enterprise

LEARNING OBJECTIVES

By the end of the chapter you should be able to:

- Understand what the inchoate offences are
- Appreciate what the inchoate offences are designed to do
- Know the *mens rea* and *actus reus* elements for the three most common statutory inchoate offences, attempt, conspiracy and s 44 of the Serious Crime Act 2007
- Appreciate that there is still a common law variety of conspiracy
- Understand the problems of impossibility in relation to inchoate offences
- Understand joint enterprise as a specific form of criminal liability and when and why it arises

INTRODUCTION

Inchoate offences are generally taught at the end of criminal law modules because an understanding of the substantive criminal offences is needed to appreciate them. The inchoates are not offences in themselves in the way that say, theft or murder are, they are a form of criminal liability and can apply to any substantive criminal offence.

Similarly, a **joint enterprise** is a way in which a crime is committed. Most criminal offences involve more than one person. If three people get together and burgle a house, then the issue of joint enterprise may become relevant.

When considering inchoate offences and the law of joint enterprise, bear in mind that the inchoate will be charged when the crime **has not** been committed for some reason, and the joint enterprise concept may become important **once the crime has taken place**.

INCHOATE OFFENCES

Key Definition

The word inchoate means 'just begun', or 'incomplete'.

These forms of offence are a very useful tool indeed for the **prosecutor**. Look down almost any charge sheet and you might see one or more of the inchoates charged as an alternative just in case the jury decide there is not enough evidence to prove beyond a reasonable doubt that the defendant actually committed the crime. There is concern in some circles about whether inchoate liability should exist at all. If we take the rationale of criminal law as being the prevention of harm, then these forms of liability are being charged and punished before the harm has occured and it might be argued in that situation, punishment is unjustifiable. This is an attractive proposition, but it depends very much on the definition of 'harm'. It also depends on the practicalities of the criminal justice sysytem. It would be ridiculous if the police – knowing that a bank robbery were due to take place at 10am on a busy Monday morning – had to wait until the offence was underway before moving in to arrest the participants, with the danger to staff and the public that would entail. Far better to arrest the gang before they get to the bank, and charge one or more of the inchoate liabilities, conspiracy to rob for instance, knowing that if convicted, defendants could be punished as if they had committed the full offence.

ATTEMPT

Attempt to commit a particular offence will be charged where the *mens rea* is in place, but for some reason the *actus reus* doesn't happen, so the harm intended isn't caused. It would, as we have said, be foolish for the law to allow a person who has put a gun to another's head and pulled the trigger to escape sanction, just because, unknown to him, the gun was loaded with blanks. However, putting a gun to a person's head and pulling the trigger is always a bad thing to do, the act is pejorative in itself, even if no physical harm is caused. What about some act that on the surface is an innocent act?

Example

Camille replaces the sugar in the sugar bowl with cyanide, meaning to kill Meera. Unbeknown to Camille, Meera's mother, Sita replaces the cyanide with sugar. When Camille makes Meera a cup of tea with two spoonfuls of sugar, she is objectively doing a kind act. Only Camille knows she is attempting to murder Meera.

This raises one of the **jurisprudential** problems of attempt as an inchoate offence, should Camille be punished for what she intended, in which case we have attempted murder, or for the dangerousness and risk to society of Camille's actions, which were making Meera a cup of tea.

Attempt is now a **statutory offence** under the Criminal Attempts Act (CAA) 1981 which abolished attempt at **common law**. Hopefully, the Act has dealt with the concerns that were raised by the common law especially as regards impossibility (see below). The CAA, s 1(4) restricts attempt to *indictable offences*. Liability for attempt of **summary offences** is only possible where such liability is included in individual statute. A person convicted of an attempted crime is liable to be punished as if the crime had been completed.

Key Definition

Section 1(1) of the CAA states:

> If, with intent to commit an offence to which this section applies, a person does an act which is more than merely preparatory to the commission of the offence, he is guilty of attempting to commit the offence.

There must be an act. A defendant cannot be charged with attempting to commit an offence which can only be committed by omission, and cannot be charged with attempting to commit an offence where the outcome is unintentional, for instance involuntary manslaughter.

Mens rea

The essence of attempt is the **intention** to commit a crime. So a charge of attempted murder is satisfied only by the intention to kill. This is important because where a substantive offence can be committed recklessly, recklessness is NOT sufficient for an attempt to commit that offence – there must be intention.

KEY CASE: *Mohan* [1976] 1 QB 1, CA

Facts:

- A man drove a car at a policeman.
- The jury were directed that the defendant could be convicted of attempt to cause actual bodily harm if he was reckless as to whether bodily harm would in fact be caused by his driving.

Held:

The conviction was quashed. Only intention to cause the harm would suffice.

Therefore, although the *mens rea* for the substantive offence of murder is the intention to kill *or* cause GBH, for attempted murder **only** intention to kill will suffice.

It seems then, that it will be harder to convict someone of attempted murder than of murder, the *mens rea* element being more rigorous. Why should this be? The emphasis in an attempted crime is very much on the *mens rea* requirement, because the *actus reus* of attempt can include actions which can seem to be entirely innocent, until they are coloured by the intention to commit the harm. Remember Camille and the cup of tea with two sugars?

Circumstances

However, recklessness as to the circumstances in which the harm is committed is sufficient for attempt, providing the same is true of the substantive offence.

KEY CASE: *Khan* [1990] 2 All ER 783

Facts:

- Khan attempted to have intercourse with a non-consenting girl.
- He was not successful but was charged with attempted rape.

- The judge at first instance said recklessness as to consent was sufficient for the charge.

Held:

The appeal against conviction was dismissed. The act here was sexual intercourse. The accused intended to penetrate the girl in the circumstances which made the sex a criminal offence, namely her lack of consent.

Recklessness as to this circumstance was a sufficient *mens rea* for the attempted crime.

Actus reus

The *actus reus* of attempt is doing an act which is 'more than merely preparatory to the commission of the offence.' This is a question of fact for the jury, who must therefore decide:

(1)   if the accused did such an act, and
(2)   whether or not that act was more than merely preparatory.

It follows then, that if a person is merely preparing to commit an offence, he cannot be guilty of attempting to commit it as the CAA 1981 requires more than preparation. Once the Criminal Attempts Act was passed, judges were urged to look first at the natural meaning of words of the statute. Unfortunately, case law is not enlightening. Consider these cases.

KEY CASES

- ***Campbell* [1991] Crim LR 268 –** the defendant was arrested outside a Post Office where he had been seen walking up and down on the pavement.
- He was carrying an imitation gun.
- He also had a balaclava to cover his face and a demand note asking for money.
- He was held to be in the act of preparing to commit the crime of robbery.
- As he had not gone beyond that stage there was no *actus reus* of attempted robbery and therefore he could not be convicted.

- ***Geddes* [1996] Crim LR 894 –** the defendant was arrested in a boy's lavatory in a school.
- He was carrying a backpack which contained a kitchen knife, masking tape and rope and a can of cider.
- Again, his actions were not advanced enough.
- He had not actually tried to commit the offence in question (kidnapping).

On-the-spot question

Bill needs money. He takes Jeremy's bank card one evening and goes along to the cash machine. There is a person in front of him using the machine, so Bill waits for his turn. Then he puts the bank card into the slot and prepares to tap in Jeremy's PIN code. At this point Bill is arrested. Could Bill be liable for attempted theft of Jeremy's money? (Theft of the card is already complete.)

Were the police to wait until Campbell had gone into the Post Office and made his demand? Did Geddes actually have to have approached a child and lay hands on him? If so, then the point of attempt – that of turning the clock back to allow for criminal sanctions before the commission of the offence could be seen to be of limited use.

KEY CASE: *Jones* [1990] 1 WLR 1057

Facts:

- The defendant followed his ex-girlfriend's new boyfriend in his car as the new boyfriend went to drop his son off at school.
- When the child left the car, the defendant jumped into the back seat of the new boyfriend's car.
- The defendant took a sawn off shotgun out from under his coat.
- He put it against the other man's head and said 'You are not going to like this.'
- It is uncertain whether or not the safety catch was off or the defendant's finger was on the trigger.

Held:

It was held that this **was** sufficient to be the *actus reus* of attempt (murder). Jones was held to have gone beyond preparatory acts and 'embarked on the crime proper'.

Note that once this point has been reached, there is no defence of withdrawal.

> **Example**
>
> Karen decides to break into a shop after it has closed for the night. She hides some tools in a hedge nearby and waits for the staff to leave. Then she retrieves the tools and begins to examine the lock on the door. At this point it seems likely that Karen has both the *mens rea* (intention) and *actus reus* (a more than merely preparatory act to the commission of the substantive offence) for attempted burglary. If Karen then decides to go home, without damaging the door or entering the shop, she will still be liable for the offence.

To recap for attempt, the *mens rea* is intention only, even if the substantive offence can be committed recklessly, and the *actus reus* is 'an act more than merely preparatory' to the commission of the substantive offence.

CONSPIRACY

A conspiracy to do something arises where two or more people agree to do it.

It should be noted that this is now a statutory offence under Criminal Law Act 1977, and the act to which the conspiracy relates has to be a criminal offence. There are also some common law offences that survived the enactment of the Criminal Law Act.

- Conspiracy to defraud.
- Conspiracy to corrupt public morals or outrage public decency. Remember the case of *Shaw* and the 'Ladies Directory'?

Therefore not quite all the conspiracy offences are under the statutory umbrella, but the basic elements discussed are the same for either statutory or common law conspiracy.

A person convicted of a statutory conspiracy is liable to a sentence of imprisonment not exceeding the maximum provided for the offence he conspired to commit. So a person convicted of conspiracy to commit theft can receive up to seven years' imprisonment.

Key Definition

Section 1(1) of the CLA 1977 states:

> if a person agrees with any other person or persons that a course of conduct shall be pursued which, if the agreement is carried out in accordance with their intentions, . . .
>
> (a)   will necessarily amount to or involve the commission of any offence or offences by one or more of the parties to the agreement, . . .
>
> he is guilty of conspiracy to commit the offence or offences in question.

The main requirement for a conspiracy, either at common law or under statute, is an agreement. For an agreement to be reached, sufficient for a charge of conspiracy, there must be a **meeting of minds,** so that the parties, however many there are, have a true agreement.

Example

Amy and Kayleigh agree to lie in wait for, and 'hurt', Adam. Amy is thinking of punching Adam and Kayleigh is thinking of killing him. If they are arrested before they ambush Adam there will be no conspiracy between Amy and Kayleigh as there is no meeting of minds here.

There are also certain parties who cannot be party to a conspiracy:

- If the only two parties to an agreement are husband and wife there can be no conspiracy, as in the case of *Mawji* [1957] AC 126.
- There is no conspiracy if the only other party is a child under 10, the age of criminal responsibility.
- There is no conspiracy where the other party is the victim of the offence, by virtue of CLA 1977, s 2(2).

KEY CASE: *Whitehouse* [1977] QB 8

Facts:

- A man was accused of conspiracy to commit incest with his daughter.
- There must be a minimum of two people for a conspiracy charge to lie.

Held:

The daughter in this case was the class of person – the child of the accused – whom the incest laws were designed to protect.

She therefore could not be charged with conspiracy to commit incest even if she had agreed with her father.

Again, it isn't enough for liability to plot to do something mentally, there has to be an agreement, voiced or written, and the offence is complete upon agreement, whether it is *express* or *implied*. However, if we are talking about pre-emptive action on crimes before any harm is committed by the individuals, this is very early on in the life of the crime. Very close in fact, to being a *mens rea* element only, the number of potential things that could happen in between two or more people honestly and earnestly planning to say rob a bank, and the actual robbing of that bank is huge. They could decide it is a silly idea, they could realise it was too risky, they could be talked out of it by a friend or a partner, they could fall out and not want to do the robbery with that person anymore or one of them could win the lottery. There are any number of reasons why that plotted offence may not take place. Yet any attempt to withdraw from the agreement after it is made will therefore bear on *mitigation* only, once the agreement is made, subject to the *mens rea* requirement, the offence is complete.

On-the-spot question

James announces loudly to a room full of people that he intends to steal money from the local bank at lunch time. Has James committed a criminal offence?

James then puts on a disguise and writes a note demanding money and walks down the High Street towards the bank. Has James committed a criminal offence? (Remember the case of *Campbell*?)

It seems that James has not yet done anything against the law, but if two of us agree to rob the bank, even if we don't take any more steps towards that end, we are guilty of conspiracy. This may seem a little unfair, but there are public policy reasons why a group of people plotting crimes is held to be more dangerous to society than a single person bent on criminality.

However, a person can be convicted of conspiracy to commit an offence which it would be impossible for them to commit as a substantive offence, for instance a female can be convicted of conspiracy to commit rape, which is a substantive crime restricted by statute to the male sex only because the requirement is for penile penetration. A person can also be convicted of conspiracy in a case where an individual is specifically exempt from the full offence.

KEY CASE: *Burns* (1973) 58 Cr App R 364

Facts:

- A father, with others, kidnapped his child from the lawful custody of the child's mother.
- The statute the others were charged under specifically excluded its use against the other parent of the child, so the father could not be charged with kidnapping his child.

Held:

He was still guilty of conspiracy to kidnap.

This case brings out one of the public policy points of conspiracy being an offence. The law is undermined when gangs of people plot crimes, and conspiracy allows all those involved in the planning to be held responsible.

Key Definition

Criminal Law Act 1977 s 5(8) and (9) state:

(8) The fact that a person or persons who, so far as appears from the indictment on which any person has been convicted of conspiracy, were the only other parties to the agreement on which his conviction was based have been acquitted of conspiracy by reference to that agreement (whether after being tried with the person convicted or

separately) shall not be a ground for quashing his conviction unless under all the circumstance of the case his conviction is inconsistent with the acquittal of the other person or persons in question.

(9) Any rule of law or practice inconsistent with the provisions of subsection (8) above is hereby abolished.

Only one conviction?

What if two people are accused of conspiracy to commit ABH, and one of them is found not guilty? Does this preclude the conviction of the other, because, of course, at least two people are needed to agree? The CLA 1977, s5 (8) and (9), says that the acquittal of one is not a bar to the conviction of the other, especially where the two are tried separately. There may, for instance be stronger proof against one, or one may have confessed and the other not.

Conspiracy isn't an offence that splits nicely into *actus reus* and *mens rea* because the *actus reus* is agreement, which contains a required state of mind within it. Look at CLA 1977, s 1(1) again to remind yourself of the elements necessary for statutory conspiracy to arise.

Contingency

If there is a contingency, such as the conspirators agreeing to only rob the bank if there are no security guards about, then if things proceed as the conspirators intend, there will be the commission of an offence – the bank will be robbed. If the conspirators arrive at the bank and find guards everywhere, so that they don't rob the bank, they will still be guilty of conspiracy.

To recap for conspiracy, the *actus reus* and the *mens rea* are somewhat difficult to separate, but there must be an agreement to a course of action, which, if carried out in accordance with the intentions of the conspirator, will amount to the commission of an offence by one or more of them.

SERIOUS CRIME ACT 2007

These offences are a little different from attempt and even from conspiracy in that it is less likely that the assister or encourager is going to be the person actually committing the crime. In the explanations below, the initial P will be used for the Principle offender, the person actually committing the crime – say murder. The initial D will be used for the person who may attract liability under s 44 – perhaps the person who lent P the gun he used to commit the murder.

Neither assisting nor encouraging are defined in the Act, which might be considered an oversight. As two words are used it is fair to imagine that they are supposed to mean different things.

Assisting

Assisting may mean the actual provision of an item or circumstance that is capable of helping the P in the commission of the crime, such as giving the P a gun to threaten someone with.

Encouraging

Encouragement seems to mean the same as the common law offence of incitement – that is conduct that includes both positive encouragement and hostile threats. So in *Marlow* [1997] Crim LR 897, a person published a book on how to grow an illegal drug, and this was held to be a positive encouragement to others to cultivate the drug, and in the case of *Goldman* [2001] Crim LR 822 a person responding to an advertisement in a magazine offering indecent images of children, was held to be inciting the placer of the advertisement to supply the pictures by virtue of his order. It is easy to see how useful these offences are at 'scooping' up persons associated with a criminal offence when they haven't quite committed it yet, but their mindset is culpable.

The SCA 2007 repealed the common law offence of incitement, under s 59 which reads:

> The common law offence of inciting the commission of another offence is abolished.

Incitement was quite a straightforward and long established concept in English law. The Serious Crimes Act 2007 replaced it with the offences of assisting and encouraging under ss 44, 45 and 46. These are a very complicated set of provisions and can only really be understood as a whole and with reference to a lot of other provisions in the SCA itself. As a result of this we are only going to be concerned with s 44 in any detail.

Key Definition

Section 44 of the SCA 2007 states:

(1) A person commits an offence if:
   (a) he does an act capable of encouraging or assisting the commission of an offence; and
   (b) he intends to encourage or assist its commission.
(2) But he is not to be taken to have intended to encourage or assist the commission of an offence merely because such encouragement or assistance was a foreseeable consequence of his act.

At first sight this looks complicated, so as always it is a good idea to break this down into *actus reus* and *mens rea* requirements.

Actus reus

There must be conduct, or a course of conduct, capable of assisting and encouraging the P. There does not have to be any actual assisting or encouraging. The P might ignore D, or not even realise what D has done. This extends previous liability under the common law offence of incitement where there had to be communication of the incitement. The *actus reus* is increased further by other sections in the act (ss 65 and 66) which say that the act is capable of assisting and encouraging P's act if it relates to a way of helping him avoid criminal proceedings, perhaps by providing a getaway car or a disguise to P. D can also be capable of 'conduct' by failing to discharge a duty by taking reasonable steps. This will be a question of fact for the jury.

Example

Vikki works as a security guard, but is asked by her friend Sean not to switch on the alarm system in the factory where she works before she goes on her patrol.

It might be argued that this is not 'conduct' on Vikki's part. Section 65(2)(b) makes it clear that in this sort of situation, Vikki's actions will be regarded as 'conduct'.

Mens rea

There are four elements of *mens rea* under s 44 and each must be proven, as well as the *actus reus* and the lack of a defence, before criminal liability results.

There must be:

1. **Intention to do the act.** There must be intention to do the act which will assist or encourage. If the act is done recklessly or negligently it will not be sufficient. If I pass you a knife knowing you are about to go on a mugging spree that is intention to assist. If I leave you in my house and you take a knife from my kitchen drawer, that may be seen as reckless behaviour on my part.

2. **Intention to assist or encourage**. The act which I do – intentionally – must be with the purpose of assisting and encouraging you. This does not include the *Nedrick/Woollin* definition of oblique intention, it is direct intention only (s 44(2)). This is a stringent *mens rea* requirement, but the inchoate offences, as we have seen, are often *mens rea* heavy to make up for the fact that they may seem to not seem to have a lot going on in the *actus reus* department.

3. **D must have a belief or be reckless as to P's *mens rea*.** This is a complicated and potentially confusing requirement. D (the assister or encourager) must believe that P (who commits the act), at the time he commits the act, will have the requisite *mens rea* for that offence

   OR D was reckless as to whether P does the act with the requisite *mens rea* OR if D did the act, he would have the requisite *mens rea*.

   The first two should be fairly straightforward, D must want P to commit the crime, so the crime must have all its elements, including *mens rea*, present when it is committed. The third is a bit less so.

   > ### Example
   >
   > Davina encourages Peter to rape Vanessa. Peter rapes Vanessa, but does not have the requisite *mens rea* because he reasonably believes Vanessa is consenting. Davina (who does not physically assault Vanessa) does have the *mens rea* for rape because she knows that Vanessa is not consenting to the penetration. Even though neither Peter nor Davina has committed rape, Davina will be convicted for assisting and encouraging rape.

4. **D must have a belief or be reckless as to the consequences or circumstances of D's offence.** If the offence assisted or encouraged has to be carried out in specific circumstances, then D must believe or be reckless as to those circumstances being in place. For example s 9 of the

Sexual Offences Act 2003 prohibits sexual activity with a child. In this offence, the circumstances are that the person with whom the sexual activity is undertaken is a child. This *mens rea* requirement is not always relevant as not all criminal offences have to be committed in specific circumstances.

Defence

There is a defence in the SCA 2007 under s 50. This is the defence of 'acting reasonably'. Again it is quite a complicated provision, but may be used, for example, if a person in a hardware shop sold a machete to a 'dodgy' looking person who went on to commit a crime using the machete. It is probably reasonable behaviour for such a shopkeeper to sell dangerous tools.

IMPOSSIBILITY

Because the inchoate offences are penalising an individual before the substantive crime has been committed and therefore before any harm has been suffered, it is easy to see that there may be situations where the crime planned, or attempted, or encouraged, could never actually have taken place, because – for one reason or another – it was impossible to do.

There are three reasons why this might be so:

1.   The result the D intends is not a crime – see below.
2.   The result the D intends will not be the crime he believes it to be – a factually impossible crime.
3.   The result the D intends cannot be achieved by the means he uses – this is referred to as 'inadequacy of means'.

Inchoate	Mistake of law	Factually impossible	Inadequacy of means
Attempt – s 1(1)b, CAA 1981	No liability	Liability possible	Liability possible
Conspiracy – s 1(2), CLA 1977	No liability	Liability possible	Liability possible
s 44, SCA 2007 – s 47(6)	No liability	Liability possible	Liability possible

As explained in the table above, the only time that impossibility is relevant to the liability of the potential defendant is when the action attempted, conspired or encouraged is not in itself a crime, in spite of a mistaken belief that it is.

> **Example**
>
> Thomas comes from a country where it is illegal to drive a car after midnight. When he comes to England, he encourages Debbie to drive at 1am, believing it to be a crime. There can be no liability for Thomas here, in spite of his intention to commit a crime, because there is – in fact – no crime here known to English law.

In all other situations, the impossibility of the substantive crime occurring is not relevant to the liability of the inchoate offender.

> **Example**
>
> Kenny conspires with Oliver to murder Jin, who, unknown to them both, is already dead. Therefore, although they both have the appropriate *actus reus* and *mens rea* for the conspiracy, the result (stabbing an already dead person!) will not be the crime that they intended. This is factual impossibility.

Where an inchoate offence is impossible due to inadequacy of means, the defendant will still be liable. As in the case above on factual impossibility, the *mens rea* and *actus reus* of the offence is still in place, in spite of the impossibility of carrying it out.

> **Example**
>
> Angelo encourages Maria to steal a bronze statue from the local park, telling her, 'It will be worth a lot of money, we could go on holiday.' Maria plans to simply pick the statue up and walk away with it one night, as she doesn't know it is much too heavy for her to lift.

The inchoate offences are simply different forms of liability for criminal offences. They are necessary to enable the state to prosecute all parties contributing to a crime, or trying to commit a crime. Joint enterprise (see below) is also a distinct form of criminal liability. Where two or more people commit a crime together, the law of joint enterprise may become relevant.

JOINT ENTERPRISE

The criminal law usually only allows a conviction when a defendant's *mens rea* is culpable. If D kills another person for example, he is not criminally liable unless he intended to kill or cause GBH. However, the principle of Joint Enterprise (JE) will sometimes hold a person responsible for a criminal action which he did not commit, and which he did not intend, or did not reasonably foresee would happen. The essence of a joint enterprise is that the participants have a 'common design'.

Example

Gwen and Geraint plan to burgle Matt's house (at this stage there would be a conspiracy to burgle). Gwen puts a knife into her bag, and Geraint says 'Why are you taking that? I don't want any trouble.' Gwen replies 'Don't worry, I won't use it – I'll just wave it about to frighten Matt if he comes home whilst we are there.' Matt comes home whilst Gwen and Geraint are in his house and Gwen stabs Matt, who dies shortly afterwards. Both Gwen and Geraint are jointly liable for murder (and burglary).

To understand why this is so, even though it seems to be unfair to Geraint, it is necessary to look at the case of *Chan Wing-sui* [1985] AC 168, JCPC.

KEY CASE: *Chan Wing-Sui* [1985] AC 168, JCPC

Facts:

- A group of men went to a flat to talk to the owner of the flat about some money he owed them (their 'common design' was to threaten him).
- The men all carried knives and knew this was so.
- One man took the owner's wife into another room so that she would remain quiet while the others talked to her husband.
- The husband was stabbed and killed.
- The defendant who had been with the wife in another room appealed against his conviction for murder, arguing that he had not known the others would stab the victim.

Held:

The court held that as long as the crime (in this case murder) was within the contemplation of the defendant as part of the joint enterprise, then he could be liable

> for the crime. He decided to continue to participate in the offence knowing that knives were being carried and therefore that they *might be* used.

If the defendants are still part of the 'common design' then all parties are liable for the outcome, even if the outcome is unforeseen as in *Chan Wing-sui*.

It is only if one of the parties steps outside of the common design (goes on a 'frolic of his own') that the other parties will not be liable for his actions. The issue of whether there is in fact a joint enterprise is for the jury to decide.

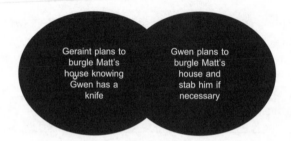

Figure 10.1

In Figure 10.1 the common design is the burglary with the weapon. Geraint must know the use of the knife by Gwen is a 'possibility'. Note the test is not even a 'probability'! The only way Geraint would not know the use of the knife was a possibility would be if Gwen did not have the knife, OR if Geraint had no idea she was carrying it. The situation above is where JE makes Geraint just a culpable as Gwen.

Figure 10.2

If Geraint does not know Gwen is carrying the knife, we have Figure 10.2, Gwen is not acting in pursuance of a JE when she stabs Matt, as there is no common purpose. There is still a JE as far as the burglary is concerned, but Geraint will not be liable for Matt's death.

From this it can be seen that for Gwen to be convicted of murder, it has to be proven beyond reasonable doubt that Gwen intended death or GBH when she stabbed Matt. For Geraint to be convicted of murder, it need only be proven that he foresaw the death or GBH as a possibility. This seems to require a higher standard of proof for the actual perpetrator of the criminal act than for the person who did not commit the *actus reus*! The policy issue behind joint enterprise liability reflects the State's concern with the problem of criminal gangs. Most crimes are committed by more than one person and if only the one that actually stole the property or assaulted another, could be held liable, there would be a big loophole in the law. The principle of JE enables that loophole to be closed.

SUMMARY

- The three most commonly charged inchoate offences are attempt, conspiracy, and assisting and encouraging an offence.
- Inchoate means 'incomplete', and these offences allow prosecution before the intended harm of the substantive offence is achieved.
- None of the inchoate offences can be charged on their own – they have to be charged as a form of liability for the offence the defendant was trying to complete – or encourage or assist another to complete.
- All three are now statutory offences, although a few common law species of conspiracy continue to exist.
- If the crime planned is impossible to commit, it does not affect the liability of the defendant unless he has made a mistake of law and the result he plans is not a crime.
- A joint enterprise will exist where the defendants have a 'common design' to commit a crime.
- While within that joint enterprise, all the parties to the common design are held responsible for any consequences of it.
- If one of the parties has a weapon and the others know about the weapon, they will be held liable if that weapon is used.

KEY CASES

Case	Legal Principle
Mohan (1976)	Intention **only** is the *mens rea* requirement for an attempted crime
Campbell (1991)	The D's actions were **not** sufficient to form the *actus reus* of attempted robbery
Jones (1990)	The D's actions **were** sufficient to form the *actus reus* of attempted murder
Mawji (1957)	There can be no conspiracy when the only two parties are husband and wife
Whitehouse (1977)	There can be no conspiracy when the only other party is the intended victim of the offence
Chan Wing-sui (1985)	All parties to a joint enterprise are liable for consequences which are foreseen as a possibility

ISSUES TO THINK ABOUT FURTHER

Should inchoate offences exist at all? It is apparent that attempt, conspiracy, and assisting and encouraging an offence are '*mens rea* heavy' offences. If there is no harm, should there be liability.

The concept of 'more than merely preparatory' is looking backwards at the crime, asking, what more would the defendant have had to do. Maybe what the law should do is look at the steps that have already been taken towards the commission of the offence. Geddes has clearly identified the school, discovered where the lavatories were, equipped himself with various items, some of which he may have had to purchase, and he clearly has the intent to commit the crime.

The inchoate offence of conspiracy can be charged much too early in the 'life' of a criminal offence. The 'public policy' rationale seems to embrace the idea that people who may plan a crime are more dangerous than those who do not.

The Serious Crimes Act 2007 is a very complicated piece of legislation, which has abolished the settled and relatively simple common law offence of incitement. It is also much broader than the offence of incitement and seems to be designed to catch those who do not in fact assist or encourage (because the P did not take any notice of them), and those who assist or encourage **after** the crime has taken place.

The principle of JE raises serious questions about the *mens rea* of the offenders. The Law Commission published a report entitled 'Participation in Crime' (Law Com No 305) which was presented to Parliament in May 2007. This report was to assist in the drafting of legislation in respect of JE. After a lengthy Parliamentary procedure the House of Commons published its response to the public consultation about the report in March 2012.

The House of Commons Justice Committee in its 11th report of session 2010/12 Vol II was concerned about the unfairness of the Joint Enterprise principle as it has developed, and warns that it condemns innocent people to long periods of imprisonment.

FURTHER READING

Ormerod and Fortson, 'Serious Crime Act 2007: the Part 2 offences' [2009] Crim LR 389 – a critique of the 2007 Act which argues that the Act is too complicated and some of the offences are unnecessary and confusing.

Rogers, 'The Codification of Attempts and the Case for "Preparation"' [2008] Crim LR 937 – a discussion of the proposed reform of the law of attempt, splitting the offence into 'criminal attempt' and 'criminal preparation'.

Editorial, 'Revising conspiracy' [2008] Crim LR 89–90 – an overview of Law Commission proposals to reform the law of conspiracy, a follow up to the editorial listed above.

Law Commission Report on Participation in Crime – available at http://lawcommission.justice. gov.uk/docs/lc305_Participating_in_Crime_report.pdf. This is a long and detailed report, but the introduction gives a comprehensive overview of the problems of joint enterprise and inchoate liability.

COMPANION WEBSITE

An online glossary compiled by the authors is available on the companion website: www.routledge.com/cw/beginningthelaw

Index